SUCCESS for TEENS®

Real Teens Talk about Using the Slight Edge®

By the **Editors** of the **SUCCESS Foundation®**

SUCCESS | BOOKS

Published by SUCCESS Books™, an imprint of SUCCESS Media™. SUCCESS Media is a division of Video Plus, L.P.

Various teen stories copyrighted by and provided courtesy of Youth Communication/N.Y. Center, Inc. See bibliography on page 143.

SUCCESS | BOOKS
200 Swisher Road
Lake Dallas, Texas 75065
U.S.A.
Toll-free: 800-752-2030
Tel: 940-497-9700
www.SUCCESS.com

200 Swisher Road
Lake Dallas, Texas 75065
U.S.A.
940-497-9700
www.SUCCESSFoundation.org

To learn more about The SUCCESS Foundation, contact us at 940-497-9700 or info@SUCCESSFoundation.org.

The Slight Edge® is a registered trademark of The Meyer Resource Group, Inc. and is used under an exclusive license.

SUCCESS is a registered trademark and SUCCESS Books is a trademark of R&L Publishing, Ltd.

SUCCESS for Teens is a registered trademark of The SUCCESS Foundation.

Video Plus is a registered trademark of Video Plus, L.P.

Printed in the United States of America.
10 9

Cover and text design by Floro Torres and Carl Waters
Copy by Jeff Olson, John David Mann, and Al Desetta

ISBN-13: 978-0-9790341-5-2
ISBN-10: 0-9790341-5-9

Contents

Preface

A MESSAGE TO TEENS

Dear Teen,

Sometimes one book can make all the difference in your life.

Stuart Johnson learned this at age 15 when he was given David Schwartz's *The Magic of Thinking Big,* which began his own personal-development journey. That book led him to read other classics, including *Think & Grow Rich* by Napoleon Hill, *Success Through a Positive Mental Attitude* by W. Clement Stone, and many others. Through these books, he discovered that working on himself first best prepared him to take on the challenges of business and life. Today, he is a highly successful businessman, the owner of VideoPlus, L.P., SUCCESS Media, *SUCCESS* magazine, and founder of the SUCCESS Foundation.

Perhaps you have received this book from a parent, coach, teacher, or friend who wants to give you a resource for making the transition from passively waiting for life to happen to actively pursuing your dreams. It is our hope that *SUCCESS for Teens* will provide you with similar "magic" for thinking big in your life.

The Slight Edge

For the past few years, I have made it my mission to help youth receive the fundamental life-skills and personal-development philosophies necessary for success in school and in life. One of the best tools I have found for achieving this is the slight edge philosophy, which was first articulated in Jeff Olson's best-selling book, *The Slight Edge.* Jeff, through his wonderful book and from more than 20 years of teaching its philosophy, has positively influenced hundreds of thousands of lives, encouraging people to do those simple, little disciplines that can change their life for the better forever.

You have in your hands what is NOT taught in high school or college. What you are now holding is the secret to a successful life. These pages provide you with the time-tested principles that will allow you to excel in all areas of your life—your health, your finances, your career, your personal relationships, and your family life. You'll learn essential skills such as goal-setting, time management, and self-motivation to help you reach new levels of achievement. And, best of all, you have the benefit of youth to get the most from these life-changing principles.

The foundation for the slight edge philosophy comes down to this: You can create any life you want, no matter how difficult it may seem, by understanding how small, positive steps make a difference over time. It's the things you do every day that don't even seem to matter... that *do* matter most. In this book, you'll learn that through the eight slight edge principles that teach you:

- ▶ Little Things Matter
- ▶ Attitude Is Everything
- ▶ You Must Use the Moment
- ▶ Everything Starts with Small Steps
- ▶ There's No Such Thing As Failure
- ▶ Habits Are Powerful
- ▶ You're Always Learning
- ▶ You Can Make Your Dreams Come True

I know that once you read these pages, you will come to understand that little things do matter, the choices you make are important, and you can make dreams come true.

Regards,

John Fleming
Executive Director
The SUCCESS Foundation
www.SUCCESSFoundation.org

A MESSAGE TO PARENTS

Dear Parent,

A startling number of young people say they aren't motivated to achieve, don't know how to plan or make decisions, and don't feel a sense of purpose.

That's why Stuart Johnson created the SUCCESS Foundation. He believes that young men and women thrive best when they first understand themselves and then apply that knowledge to the world around them. He wanted a way to illustrate the importance of clarifying goals, practicing the small efforts necessary for success, and accepting responsibility for one's own destiny.

We believe that every teen needs to be directed toward a path that enables them to achieve their goals, pursue careers, and become productive citizens. The tools for enhancing skills such as goal setting, dream-building, self-motivation, time management, and creating high self-esteem and a sense of purpose are so very important but often not taught in school. The SUCCESS Foundation believes that providing today's youth with personal development resources such as *SUCCESS for Teens* will help them reach their full potential.

I encourage you to share the fundamental life-skills and personal-development philosophies found in these pages and at www.SUCCESSFoundation.org with your teen. Together, we can help make a difference in the lives of our children.

Regards,

John Fleming
Executive Director
The SUCCESS Foundation
www.SUCCESSFoundation.org

Foreword

FROM THE DAUGHTER:
Small Steps Win the Race

The slight edge has made a huge and positive impact on my life, and it can do the same for you.

When I was a senior in high school, I felt overwhelmed about applying to college. Applications, essays, recommendations, financial aid—there are tons of things I had to get together, and I felt the pressure to do it better than anyone else. I didn't think I would ever get everything done, but I ended up putting together a strong application and getting into colleges that I wanted. How did that happen? Because I disciplined myself in getting everything ready and didn't leave anything for the last minute. I didn't let my feelings of being overwhelmed keep me from accomplishing tasks. I applied the slight edge—I took one small step after another until I reached my goals.

My most vivid memory of how I used the slight edge was during my freshman year at the University of Florida. There were about 8,000 students in the freshman class, and everyone was incredibly smart and had done great things in high school. Once again I felt overwhelmed, up against people who were obviously very bright. I wasn't sure I belonged among them.

I remember asking my dad, Jeff Olson, "How am I going to do well in college? How am I going to stand out?"

And he gave me some fantastic advice: "If you apply the slight edge principles, simply show up at your classes every day, and do the things your professors tell you to do, you're going to beat 50 percent of the people by just doing that."

What my father meant was that many people just don't put in the effort—they let the small things go by the wayside. So starting out freshman year, I went to classes every day and studied every night. It was amazing to me how many students didn't do those small things—instead, they crammed for tests and tried to take shortcuts at the last minute.

I did very well in college and graduated in the top 15 percent of my class. It wasn't because I was smarter than the other 85 percent of my classmates—it was because I was disciplined and did the small things every day, the little things that didn't look like such a big deal at the time.

Life is always a struggle, and you can get in the mindset that skipping the small things and taking shortcuts isn't going to harm you, especially when you get to college, because the professors aren't checking up on you, making sure you read the books, and showing up to class. You're on your own, and you can end up thinking, "If I don't go to class one day, it isn't going to hurt me." But the little things you do every day are more important than you can imagine.

Whether you want to play a new sport, do better in math, lose five pounds, or write your own book, the slight edge philosophy will help you. Success *will* come your way, if you do the things that are simple and small, and do them every day. You don't need to take huge leaps in life. When you tackle problems and challenges step by step, you'll be amazed at how much progress you can make.

Remember the tortoise and the hare—slow and steady wins the race. I wish you the best of luck on your journey.

Amber Olson
Dallas, Texas

FROM THE DAD:
When I Was 19, I Was Headed Nowhere

I wish someone had given me this book when I was a teen. I sure could have used it.

For the first 20 years of my life, *success* was the last word anyone would have used to describe me. Throughout my childhood and teen years, it seemed like I was destined for nothing but failure and trouble.

In the third grade my teachers told me I had a low I.Q. My dad died when I was 10, and I became a troublemaker. My mom did her best to hold everything together, but as a fatherless, blond-haired kid growing up in a Hispanic neighborhood in Albuquerque, New Mexico, I just didn't fit in. I struggled my way through school, and by the time I was 19, I was headed nowhere.

But somewhere along the way I stumbled upon the ideas in this book—and everything shifted.

I went to college, got straight A's, and graduated at the top of my class. I went to work for a company and did well, then left and started my own company, which became one of the largest in its field. Then I built another company. Since then, I've created several multimillion-dollar sales organizations, produced nearly 1,000 television programs with *New York Times* best-selling authors, and presented seminars in every major city in the United States. I've even written a best-selling book, called *The Slight Edge,* upon which this book is based.

I don't want you to get the wrong idea here: This book is not just about financial and career achievements. Success is not defined by money. It's about what you achieve in *all* areas of your life. Beyond the business successes and bank accounts, I've been blessed with the joys of family and friends. I have relationships in my life that are more fulfilling than I ever thought possible. I've discovered new ways of learning and taken many paths to adventure.

When I was 19, it looked like I was getting ready to flunk out of life. But today I have an amazing life, one I never could have imagined when I was a teen. None of this was luck, and it sure wasn't coincidence. I owe it all to the ideas contained in the pages you're about to read.

"The slight edge philosophy comes down to this: you can create any life you want—*but not all at once, and only by utilizing your philosophy and the secret of time*. To understand that little steps, compounded over time, *do* make a difference. That the things you do every single day—the things that don't look dramatic, that don't even look like they matter—*do* matter."

I learned this in my 20s, but now you have the opportunity to learn in just a few hours the valuable principles that took me years to learn. I've seen it work wonders for my daughter Amber, for her friends, and for other teens. You can put these principles to work no matter how old you are, and the earlier you start, the better.

I am honored that The SUCCESS Foundation, which made it possible for you to be holding this book in your hands, has built its first initiative around the slight edge principles that have changed so many lives. It is a most important endeavor, and I applaud and support my good friend Stuart Johnson for his commitment to providing teens with the personal development tools and resources needed to achieve new levels of success.

As I said before, I wish someone had given me this book when I was a teen. Fortunately, you won't have that same regret, because someone who cares about you has put it in your hands *now*. My deepest wish is that you read it, take it to heart and put it into practice.

Here's to your amazing life!

Jeff Olson
Author, *The Slight Edge*

Introduction

LITTLE THINGS MATTER

This book is about becoming the best possible person you can be. It's about making the most of your talents and opportunities, dealing with problems in positive ways, no matter what life brings, and achieving success—however you define it.

We've talked to teens from around the country to find out how they define success and what they're doing to make their dreams come true. And the answers they gave seem to boil down to the same answer (or set of answers).

Teens have said that success in life is not a question of how smart you are, how talented you are, or how lucky you are. It's not about the family you come from, the neighborhood you grew up in, or the school you go to. It's not about good looks or good luck.

There's only one difference between teens who are on the path to success, and those who aren't yet on the path.

That difference is called the slight edge and it boils down to three words: *Little things matter.*

Or, to put it another way, you can create any life you want—but not all at once, and only by taking small, positive actions every day. These small steps may not look like a big deal, but the teens in this book show how important they really are. By understanding your attitudes and the secret of time, you can achieve success in life, no matter how difficult that might seem right now. The slight edge is having faith that miracles do happen, if you know how to trust yourself and keep trying.

To understand the heart of the slight edge, let's look at an example from nature.

THE LESSON OF THE WATER HYACINTH

The water hyacinth is one of the most beautiful and unusual plants on earth. A delicate flower with six petals, it ranges in color from blue to lavender to pink and floats on the surface of ponds in warm areas around the world.

What makes the water hyacinth really special is that it is one of the fastest-growing plants in the world. A single water hyacinth can produce as many as 5,000 seeds and sends out short stems that become new plants. Over time, a single water hyacinth continuously doubles itself—one plant becomes two plants, two plants become four plants, four plants become eight plants, and so on.

One day there was a very beautiful (and very small) water hyacinth growing near the edge of a big pond. Nobody noticed it. Nobody noticed the second day either, when it had doubled and there were now two plants. Nobody noticed the water hyacinths on the third day or the fourth day. Even though they kept doubling in numbers, the water hyacinths were so small on the big pond that you'd have to look very hard to see them.

For two weeks the water hyacinths continued to double, but still covered only one square foot of the pond, just a tiny part of its huge surface. On Day 20, a person passing by the pond noticed something floating along the shore, but mistook it for a lost towel or a discarded trash bag. But by Day 30, it was impossible to ignore the hyacinths, because a blanket of beautiful flowers now covered the pond's entire surface.

The lesson of the water hyacinth is this: Small actions may not seem like much at first, but over time they have a compounding effect. All that means is that actions add up or intensify over time—you can get big results from small, daily steps. This is perhaps the most important lesson of the slight edge and it applies directly to your life.

As you read this book, keep the image of the water hyacinth in your mind. You are making choices every day, every hour of your life, and the impact of those choices spreads throughout your life like a blanket of water hyacinths covering a pond. You may not see the results of your choices today, tomorrow, or even next year. But, over time, you *will* see the results of your actions.

The question is this: What kinds of actions will you choose?

As you read on, remember two more important points.

- Only you can define what success means, and no one can do it for you. It's what you most want to do, not what others tell you to do.
- Everyone has the ability to be successful. Maybe you think success comes only from doing incredibly difficult things—things you don't think you'll ever be able to do. But that's simply not true.

The teens in this book talk about the many ways they've used the slight edge:

- They describe how they discovered what matters most in life, and how that's influenced their decisions and choices.
- They will teach you new ways of thinking and acting that will help you to make wise choices, whether at home, with friends, in school, in choosing a career, or in using your talents to their fullest potential.
- They will show you how to deal with difficult obstacles and challenges and keep going until you reach your goals.
- They will explain how you can be successful, however you define it.

Listen to what these teens have to say. Think about your own life as they tell their stories. After each story, ask yourself some questions. How are their experiences similar to yours? How are they different? How can you use what they've learned to improve your life? What new ideas or insights do you have? (If you want, there are places in the book where you can write down your thoughts and reactions.)

But most of all, use the advice these teens have to share—because, if you do, your life will start to change. Maybe not tomorrow or even the next day, but soon enough. Because when you understand the slight edge, time is on your side.

Little Things Matter

When Ferentz Lafargue was 16, he thought back to the fun he had with his friends when he was younger. They hung out in a parking lot, playing baseball, football, manhunt, and anything else they could think of. Like most kids, they made up their own games.

One day we noticed a piece of wood in the corner of the lot. We found a rock to prop it up and made ourselves a bicycle ramp. We practiced jumping for a week or two until the wood broke.

Every winter when it snowed, there would be huge piles of snow in the corners of the lot. We would start out by doing some light skiing to get warmed up. (The skis were made of the finest cardboard we could find.) But we all know what happens when you put a bunch of guys somewhere with snow... SNOWFIGHT!! When that happened, it was every man for himself. We would go home looking like we had just climbed Mt. Everest, and sometimes I think that would have been easier.

But Ferentz and his friends drifted apart:

These days the parking lot is just used for parking cars. We don't even keep in touch like we used to. Rarely will you see two of us together. Some have moved away, the rest just feel like they're miles away. The only thing we all have in common is that we grew up.

Devon was the superstar of the parking lot. He could throw, run, catch—the whole nine. We thought he would play high school base-ball or football, and go on to become a major leaguer. But instead he ended up hanging out and doing things like robbing people, stealing chains, or getting caught up in stupid gang battles. Devon's only 18 and has been sent to jail two times already. The sad thing is he has no fear of going back.

Devon's younger brother John was a pretty good ballplayer, too, but more importantly he was a B+ student and a born leader. Now John is 17 and has a kid, and he's not even close to a high school diploma. He was hardly ever in school last year. The word is that John is dealing guns.

Then there's Angel, who used to be my best friend and in a way he always will be. One summer he lost his glove and, being that he was the only lefty in the parking lot, he taught himself to pitch right-handed. He could trick an opposing batter with a wicked right-handed curve ball.

Angel hasn't dropped out yet, but I doubt he goes to school more than five full days a year. He's dealing drugs. He used to have determination, but these days the only thing he seems determined to do is mess up his life.

I looked up to Devon and John and Angel. But I was smart enough to learn from their mistakes. I intend to go to college and study communications and advertising. One day, hopefully, I'll be writing for a big-time newspaper or working for an advertising company. Then I'd like to do whatever I can to help out some of my old friends.

Devon, John, and Angel still keep an eye out for me. Every time one of them sees an article I've written or hears about me doing anything else good, he's always ready to congratulate me and tell me to keep it up. It's almost like I'm their last hope of success: If I come out OK, then they'll honestly be able to say they had a hand in raising me.

Perhaps you've known people as talented as Devon, John, and Angel. Any of them could have turned their skills in a better direction. Why didn't they? Because of three words: *Little things matter.*

POINT #1: LITTLE THINGS MATTER

Those three words are the heart of this book. The slight edge is a pretty basic idea and you can sum it up this way: every day, every hour, every moment of your life, you face a choice. You can take a simple, positive action. Or you can take a simple, negative action. The difference between teens who feel successful and those who don't feel that way comes from the little choices they make about what they think, say, and do.

Simple actions, repeated over time, will determine the life you lead. Devon, John, and Angel didn't become dropouts involved in crime and drugs overnight. They made small choices, day after day, week after week, until they lost their way. That's the bad news. The good news is that everyone—even people who seem as lost as Devon, John, and Angel—can start making different choices today and turn their lives around. It's never too late to change.

The little things that lead to success are easy to do. They can be as simple as getting up on time in the morning, showing up at school, and doing homework. The steps can be very small—as small as choosing a different response in the moment.

> The slight edge is a pretty basic idea. Whenever you face a choice, you can take a simple, positive action. Or you can take a simple, negative action. Simple actions, repeated over time, will determine the life you lead.

Mikaela Suarez, 13, from Rogers, Arkansas, likes to stay in the back of the class during dance class. She doesn't like the attention up front.

One day my friend asked me if I wanted to stand up closer to the teacher and I said, "No, I'm fine where I am." But my teacher overheard and asked me to stand up front. During that whole class I was really mad at my friend. But I didn't say anything and instead focused on dancing. And that was a positive decision on my part, to not get mad or worry about what anyone was thinking.

Octavia Fugerson, 17, from Atlanta, Georgia, went into foster care when she was 15 and was very depressed, to the point where she sometimes thought of suicide. But she now plans to become a psychologist and someday have her own foster care agency staffed by former foster kids. What enabled her to deal with her pain and stick to her goals?

I always looked for positive distractions. I knew if I got involved in drugs it wouldn't help me, only bring me down more. I tried to distract myself through reading and writing. If I was having a real rough day, I would just read a book to distract me away from everything and take me to another world. Writing poetry also helps me. I can't honestly say that it takes the load off, but it helps me understand it, which takes the load off indirectly.

Small actions compound over time. For example, if you exercise for an hour a day, you won't see much difference after a couple days or even a week. But after a couple of months you'll notice a big difference. A little effort each day will result in huge rewards over time.

Kyle Freas, 19, from Plano, Texas, found himself with too much time on his hands.

I used to play basketball every day after school. I was on the school team. When the season was over, I had like three extra hours every day, because I was still in the habit of using that time to play basketball. I always wanted that extra time, but then when I had it I didn't know what to do with it.

So Kyle began spending an hour a day looking for ways to help other kids. In the last seven years he's raised thousands of dollars to help abused, homeless, and sick children. And Kyle considers himself just an average kid.

People get the idea that I'm not a normal teenager, that I don't have friends, that my project is all I do. I'm a normal kid with normal friends. I play video games and sports. I'm nothing special. It doesn't take anything spectacular to have an influence like I've had. I just put in a little effort every day.

Mikaela, Octavia, and Kyle, each in their own way, used the slight edge:

▸ Mikaela chose to remain silent when she was angry instead of lashing out at her friend.
▸ Octavia turned to reading or writing when she was depressed.
▸ Kyle spent an hour a day on a new project.

The little things they did weren't so little after all.

Think about how this applies to your own life. For example, if you exercise for an hour a day, you won't see much difference after a couple days or even a week. But after a couple of months you'll notice a big difference. If you read 10 pages of a good book every day, it might not seem like a lot. But after one year, you'll have read more than two-dozen 150-page books. It's the same with learning to play a new instrument or improving at a sport. A little practice each day will result in huge rewards over time.

Taylor, 18, discovered how small actions compound over time as she played soccer. She has a passion for the sport and has played it since she was 5 years old. But the older she got, the more competitive the sport got. Although Taylor loves soccer, she's never liked running. And soccer is a sport that demands a lot of running. When she was 15, her trainer made Taylor's soccer team practice extra running drills.

> We had practice three times a week, and the first hour of it was conditioning. And then on the days when we didn't have practice our coach told us to go out and run three miles. And we had to be able to run those three miles in 30 minutes.
>
> For the entire first month, I couldn't even finish the three miles. I would stop at two and a half because the pain was so great. It made me sick to my stomach to run that far. It was blazing hot outside, because I'm in South Texas. And there would be days when I wouldn't run because I didn't feel like it.
>
> I thought maybe I could get away with not doing it. But when I would show up at practice the next day, you could tell who ran and who didn't. When I started to look like someone who was slacking, I realized that it was bigger than just me. I needed to help the team. I needed to do my part in order to make a difference.
>
> I had friends encouraging me. They told me, "We want to do well at the end of the season. If you love this sport, then you need to do what it takes to honor your commitment to it."
>
> So on the days I didn't feel like running, I would make myself put on my tennis shoes and go outside and do it. Even if I had to start slow, I realized I was at least trying instead of sitting at home.

At the start I knew I couldn't run three miles in 30 minutes, so I told myself I'll do what I can and see how that goes. The first day I could do only two miles in 30 minutes. It was slow and painful because I hadn't been running. But once I kept going I could see myself getting faster, and once you see yourself getting faster the easier it gets. It took me two months to run the three miles in 30 minutes.

During the soccer season, coaches who were looking for college players scouted Taylor's high school team.

Coaches would send me e-mails, saying, "I noticed you played the entire game, and it's really impressive to see girls who can last that long on the field and not show any wear and tear, to be able to play 100 percent the entire time." It was an eye opener to get these e-mails from college coaches who noticed how I could run so much, when a few months before I couldn't even run three miles.

Taylor is now attending college on a scholarship and playing for the school team.

Small actions compound over time. That means they grow in size and impact and lead to much bigger things. This is one of the most important lessons of the slight edge.

ACTION STEPS
- What small steps could you take to reach your goals?
- What steps could you start taking today?

POINT #2: KNOWING WHAT TO DO ISN'T THE SAME AS DOING IT

Teens we spoke to said that knowing how to do something and actually doing it are two different things. For example, Angel, Devon, and John had the talent and intelligence to know the right things to do, but still ended up making the wrong choices.

Knowing how to do something isn't actually doing the thing. Having the answer to a problem isn't the same thing as using the answer to solve the problem. That's because the little things that are important to do are also easy *not* to do, so a lot of people don't do them.

You know this from your own life. What's easier—trying something you're afraid of, or not even trying in the first place? Going along with what others think, or being who you really are, even if it means feeling alone? Avoiding your feelings because they're too hard or painful to face, or facing them square on? Getting up and running in the morning, or sleeping late?

The answer is pretty clear—it's often a *whole lot* easier not to do the simple things.

Some teens told us they didn't do the little, positive things because of what other people thought. Jesselin Rodriguez, 16, faced this problem when she got into junior high. It wasn't cool to be a success in school. If you did well, you got teased. Failure was cool—not in the sense that everyone fails at one time or another and can learn from it, but in the sense that it was cool to not do your best and be stuck in failure forever.

> *When I was in elementary school, doing well in school was the only thing that mattered to me. But when I got to junior high that all changed.*
>
> *The atmosphere in junior high was totally different. When I walked in there for the first time, it seemed like everyone was just chillin'. I saw kids hanging out in the auditorium when they didn't belong there and even screaming at teachers. There was a fight almost every day. No one seemed to care about classes.*
>
> *In that school you looked crazy if you were doing any work. The important thing was to have friends. If you didn't have friends, you were nothing. You'd get picked on, cursed out, and if people fought you it was never one-on-one.*
>
> *I decided schoolwork wasn't going to be my top priority anymore. I thought my classmates would like me better if I acted more like them— lazy and not caring about anything except going home to watch TV.*
>
> *So I made it a point to have friends and started thinking of school as a playground. I could do anything there—cut classes, write on the walls,*

hide in the bathrooms—and nobody knew about it because there were too many kids.

When I did go to class, I'd walk in 20 minutes late, sit with a friend, and talk the rest of the period away. When the teachers asked me why I was late, I told them that I was in the bathroom or that I was talking to another teacher about something. They wouldn't bother me after that.

I did just enough work to pass, but I made it a point to never let my friends find that out. On the days when I did my homework, I used to give it to the teacher after class so my friends wouldn't see. If they knew, I was sure they would give me a hard time. They would be like, "What are you doing the work for? You think you're better than us?"

Then my class was divided up. The kids with the worst behavior and grades, including most of my friends, were sent to a different class. Since I didn't have my crew to do things with anymore, I had two choices—I could either not go to school at all, or I could start doing my work.

I knew my mother would kill me if I didn't go to school, so I started to go to class every day and began to do my homework on a more regular basis. My teachers were happy, and so was I.

By the time I was in eighth grade, I had worked my way up to a B average. I still felt that I could do better, but I didn't want to get higher grades than most of the people in my class. I thought they would get mad at me and be like, "Oh, now she thinks that she's smarter than me."

Soon Jesselin started high school.

Then came ninth grade and a big reality check. I thought that high school was going to be a bigger playground than junior high. I was wrong. Even though most of the kids were the same, the atmosphere was very different.

It was a brand-new alternative school and there were only about 50 students in the whole place. Every teacher knew who you were and where you were supposed to be every minute of the day. I had to do my work because there was no place to hide.

My teachers knew that I was smart and saw right through my front of acting like I didn't care. Still, I thought that as long as I handed in a couple *of pieces of work they would be satisfied and not bother me. For my whole freshman year, I was constantly told that I could do better. But it just went in one ear and came out the other.*

Over the summer after ninth grade, I was talking to a friend who was in college. He asked me how I was doing in school. I told him that I was doing OK.

"How OK?" he asked. I told him I was doing just enough to pass. He asked me why, because he knew I could be at the top of my class if I wanted to be. I told him that I had gotten very lazy.

Then he asked me if I wanted to go to college. I told him that what I really wanted was to get a scholarship so I could go to a college out of state.

My friend told me there was no way I was going to get a scholarship. He even told me to forget about college at all, because I probably wouldn't finish high school the way I was going.

He put so much fear in me that I spent the rest of that summer thinking about what he said. It was the same thing my teachers had been telling me for years. It finally started to sink in. For a long time, it had been my dream to be the first one in my family to graduate from high school and go to college. Now I realized that I was going to have to work to make that dream come true.

Jesselin began to change.

For all of 10th grade, I did nothing but work. Breaking my lazy habits was the hardest thing I have ever done. I had to get used to doing my homework every night, not just when I felt like it. And I had to make a lot of sacrifices. I couldn't sit home and watch TV all day. I hardly listened to music. And I didn't see a lot of my friends outside of school. They would say, "Jesse, let's go downtown so I can go buy this shirt" or, "Let's go downtown and just chill." And I was always saying, "No, I can't, I have to stay after school and finish my work."

So, here I am, a junior almost ready for college—not at all ashamed of how bright I am, and not caring who knows it. It feels like the good girl I once had inside me has come back.

Jesselin learned that success can mean going against what's popular and sacrificing for what you really want. She started doing the little, positive things even when she didn't feel like it. She started to believe in herself and in what she knew was most important. And she started using that knowledge, even if other people were telling her something different. Instead of just knowing the right things to do, Jesselin actually did them. And she grew as a person and made herself a better life.

ACTION STEPS

- Is there something you know you should be doing that you're not doing?
- What's stopping you from taking that small, positive step?

POINT #3: THE RIPPLE EFFECT

You've heard the expressions "timing is everything" or "he was in the right place at the right time." What that means is that by doing the small, positive things, you increase the chances that other positive things will happen to you. It's like tossing a rock into a pond—you'll see a splash and the ripples spreading out, but those ripples can go far beyond what you see. They can go all the way to the opposite shore.

It's the same thing in life, although you often don't see the ripples until something good happens (or something not so good). For better or for worse, even your smallest actions create a ripple effect that has a huge impact on you and the people around you, even when you don't see it or aren't aware of it.

Jordan Schwartz, 14, of Marietta, Georgia, knows from experience that when you do a simple, positive thing, you never know where it will lead. A few years ago she was traveling with her family and passing through an airport.

There was a woman there who had lost all her travel papers and she didn't speak one word of English. She was Spanish-speaking. My mother, who speaks Spanish, noticed something was going on and went over and offered her services. And she helped the woman get her forms filled out and on her way. It was all done in about a half-hour, with my mom stepping up to the plate, when it would have taken an hour with a translator.

That incident made a big impact on Jordan, because it made her think about helping others.

Some people think that community is just your town or your city. It's bigger than that—a sense of community means a sense of right and wrong, a sense of what to do in certain situations.

Jordan kept thinking about what happened in the airport when she got home. At the time she was raising money for a local police canine unit. She just wanted to donate the money, but the police commissioner invited her to make a speech about her project.

After it was over, the commissioner thanked me, said I did a great job, and said if I ever needed anything in the future to please let him know. So I took him up on his word.

When you do small, positive things, it increases the chances that other positive things will happen to you. Your smallest actions affect you and the people around you, even when you don't see it or aren't aware of it.

Ever since her mother helped the Spanish-speaking woman, Jordan had been thinking about people's attitudes about bilingualism, or speaking more than one language. Some people in her community think it's great that people speak Spanish in this country, while others think Americans should only speak English. Like her mother, Jordan speaks both English and Spanish, and she decided to start a bilingual theater for children to teach tolerance and acceptance of everyone, no matter what language they speak. When the police commissioner asked if she needed anything, she told him about her idea and asked for his help.

The commissioner helped Jordan get permission to use school auditoriums to stage her productions. And that started her theater project on its way.

I was sending e-mails and putting flyers in the windows of local shops and businesses. After about a week or two of that, I started getting calls from people who wanted to help.

Today, Jordan's project—called the Children's Bilingual Theater—puts on several theater productions each year, in both English and Spanish, involving more than 100 young people.

And it happened because of the ripple effect:

▶ Jordan's mother helps a stranger in an airport.
▶ Jordan thinks about the meaning of community and starting a theater project.
▶ She's already working on another community project and an adult offers to help Jordan with anything she needs.
▶ With his help, Jordan starts her theater project.
▶ Soon the word spreads and other people are pitching in to help.

When you take a small, positive step, you never know where it will lead. But if you take that first step, the chances are great that more positive things will happen to you.

ACTION STEPS

● Have you seen the ripple effect in your own life?
● Have you ever taken a positive step that led to another positive thing for you?

POINT #4: MAKE THE RIGHT CHOICE AT THE RIGHT MOMENT

Only you can define what success means. But however you define it, the slight edge basically means doing the right thing at the right moment. That's where it all starts, and that often takes a lot of courage.

Chantel Clark understands this. When she was a senior in high school, Chantel hated a girl named Kim.

> Kim was dark-skinned, with short hair she often wore in braided extensions. She was loud for no good reason and would get nasty with you in a heartbeat! She didn't care what people thought or said, dressing how she wanted regardless of trends.
>
> Kim and I had different styles, but we were also a lot alike, and we found each other threatening because of that. In freshman year we got into a fight. She started it, over some "he-said, she-said." I won and gained my peers' respect.
>
> After that, I had to live up to my reputation. So when I walked past her, I had nothing to say. If we saw each other in the mall, we would roll our eyes at each other. If we saw each other at a party, we made it our business to walk past each other with disgust.
>
> But when I came back to school from summer vacation senior year, I saw my archenemy and she was no longer the same. Kim didn't do her hair or dress nice anymore. She didn't even hang out with her group of friends. I began to see people picking on her for no reason, calling her names, throwing things at her, and starting fights.
>
> I heard through people that Kim was homeless because her mom kicked her out. She was getting skinny, her face looked like death and, honestly, I was worried. For the first time I did not want to pick an argument with her.

Chantel's attitude toward Kim began to change:

> I know pain firsthand, and it's weird—once you've been hurt or gone through some trials, it's like you know when someone else is hurting inside. You can sense it, you can feel it. I had a yearning inside to talk to Kim, because I was sure I could speak to her like no one else could.
>
> One day I went to the office of the school social worker, Ms. Bee, and saw Kim crying. I felt a heaviness in my chest. I wanted to reach out to her, but I couldn't.
>
> I was scared about talking to her. What would people think? I also thought to myself, "What if I try to be nice and this chick gets smart? I might curse her out." So my pride, my temper, and my attitude kept me still.

I left Ms. Bee's office wondering what I could do. How could I speak to Kim? What would she say?

I returned to Ms. Bee's office later that day and asked her what was wrong with Kim, but she knew our rivalry and said it was confidential. So I asked Ms. Bee if she could set up a meeting between Kim and me. I explained that I saw how much pain she was in and wanted to help in any way I could.

Ms. Bee knew my life story and that I would be able to say things that only the two of us could have understood.

> However you define success, the slight edge basically means doing the right thing at the right moment. That's where it all starts, and that often takes a lot of courage.

About a week or so later, Ms. Bee called me into her office, and Kim was there. I suddenly felt out of place and weird, but I went in anyway.

I said to Kim, "I came from a broken home, my life was never a bowl of cherries. My mother, a drug abuser. My father, missing in action. No one knew when he would pop up. But I was strong enough to overcome. You're beautiful and strong, and if you ever need a shoulder to cry on, I'm here."

Kim was shocked. She looked at me with this face that said, "No way." I guess she never saw me as the type to have a hard life, because I hide it so well.

I told her how this fairy princess in a glass castle is my image, but it's only a lie. We told each other things that almost nobody knew, and we laughed about it, too. After that conversation we became true friends, because we trusted each other. People often stared at us and talked behind our backs, because we were once enemies but are now friends. They could never understand the relationship we had.

I gave her clothes, lent her money, and snuck her into my house to eat and to hang out. We became like sisters.

We realized we could both change and be our real selves. She didn't need to be loud to be respected. I found out that I didn't have to pretend all the time. I could be me without worrying about what anyone else would think. I helped Kim to find herself again and in return I found me.

Success is more than finding the right job someday or making a lot of money. It's about doing the right thing at the right time.

That takes faith and courage. Chantel had faith in knowing the right thing to do and the courage to do it. Once you start using the slight edge, you will have both faith and courage to make the right choices.

Think About It

What Does Success Mean to You?

What does success mean to you? To find out, start with these questions:

- ✎ What's important to you?

- ✎ What do you like to do?

- ✎ What do you care about?

- ✎ What things mean the most to you?

After you've thought a while, jot down your thoughts in the spaces below.

What are five things you're good at? List them here:

_____

_____

_____

_____

_____

Now, what are five things you love to do, whether or not you're especially good at them? (You may end up listing some or all of the same things in your first list. That's OK.)

_____

_____

_____

_____

_____

And now, let's take it a step further, too: What are five things you would

do if you could, no matter how outrageous they are, even if you think you're no good at them?

_____

_____

_____

_____

_____

Is there something you would have included on that last list, but didn't because it seemed too far-fetched? Maybe even impossible? If so, write it down here.

_____

_____

_____

_____

_____

This gives you a pretty good idea of how you define success. But how are you going to get there? By taking small steps. So let's take the next step.

Success Starts with Little Steps

Think of three little things you can do that could lead to success in six areas of your life. Then write them down below. (Remember—they can be small steps! And you can repeat what you've written above in the spaces below.)

For Myself:

1. _____

2. _____

3. _____

For My Friendships:

1. _____
2. _____
3. _____

For My Health (physical, mental, and spiritual):

1. _____
2. _____
3. _____

For My Wealth:

1. _____
2. _____
3. _____

For My Education and Career:

1. _____
2. _____
3. _____

For My Footprint on the World (what I want to accomplish or how I want to be remembered):

1. _____
2. _____
3. _____

Hold onto your answers—we'll come back to them. But in the meantime, which of these steps can you take today?

Attitude Is Everything

L ittle things matter. But what makes you do the little things, whether positive or negative? Have you ever thought about that?

It's not willpower that determines what you do. Willpower means forcing yourself to do something you don't really want to do. You can't force yourself to enjoy washing the dishes or raking the yard or helping your brother with his homework if you don't really feel like it. That may work for a while, but not for long. You can't keep forcing yourself to do something if you don't really want to do it.

No, it's not willpower that drives your actions, but your attitude.

Your attitude shows itself in everything you do. Your attitude is so powerful that people can sense it before you say a word. Your body language conveys your attitude—you can sense how someone feels by the way he or she walks down the street, enters a room, or sits on a couch. Your attitude determines both your simplest and most complicated actions—from the way you carry yourself to the way you deal with hard times.

So, is controlling your attitude the "secret" to controlling your actions? If you could control your attitude, then you'd be able to control your actions, right?

Not exactly. That doesn't work because you don't have one single attitude. Your attitudes are changeable. One day you couldn't be happier—until you run into your ex-boyfriend or ex-girlfriend at school, or your mother yells at you, or you get teased again in the

> Your attitude determines both your simplest and most complicated actions—from the way you carry yourself to the way you deal with hard times.

lunchroom. Maybe today you're excited about studying for that upcoming test. And because you feel like it, you crack the books and get moving on it. But what if you just don't feel like studying tomorrow? Then what?

Your attitude is changing all the time. And as your attitude changes, your feelings also change. Some days you're not going to feel great. And it's hard, if not impossible, to just force yourself to feel happy when you're not.

The key to how your life turns out is your ability to understand the source of your attitude. And the source of your attitude is your philosophy—the way you see yourself and the way you see the world.

Trying to control your attitude and feelings might work at first, but not for long.

So if your actions are not a result of willpower, determination, or controlling your attitude and feelings, then what *is* at the heart of your actions?

POINT #1: YOUR PHILOSOPHY IS THE KEY

The key to the slight edge, or doing the little, positive things, is discovering the *source* of your attitude. Understanding what's at the heart of what you feel and believe is the key to achieving what you want in life. It comes down to what is called your "philosophy," which is a fancy word for the way you see yourself and the way you see the world.

ACTION STEPS
- Have you thought about the source of your attitudes?
- Do you feel you understand them?
- What could you do to better understand your attitudes?

POINT #2: HOW YOU VIEW YOURSELF CREATES YOUR LIFE

Whether you know it or not, you already have a philosophy. Maybe you've never put it into words. Maybe you've never even noticed it, much less thought about it. But you have one. Everyone does.

Remember, all "philosophy" means is your view of life or your picture of how life operates. Your philosophy is *how you see things*. Your philosophy is what determines your attitudes and your actions, whether you realize it or not.

your philosophy —> your attitudes

your attitudes —> your actions

your actions —> your life

Your philosophy is more important than just having book information or knowledge. Your philosophy is the secret that lies behind the puzzle of fate and destiny. Two people will grow up in the same difficult family or rough neighborhood, but one person will overcome it and the other won't. Why?

Because how they *view* their experiences will determine how they *react* to them.

You create your destiny with your actions. But your actions are determined by your attitudes, and your attitudes in turn are determined by how you see the world.

Sometimes you get pulled away from your philosophy when you're confronted by a difficult choice or challenge. This happened to Sage, 18.

When I was 16, it turned out that my friends were smoking weed, and I thought they were really stupid. Then, as usual, I started questioning myself—I wondered if they were having a lot of fun. So I took a little puff, and it was no fun at all. In fact, it hurt my lungs.

> You create your destiny with your actions. But your actions are determined by your attitudes, and your attitudes result from how you see the world— by your philosophy.

*I thought it was stupid, gave it a little try, confirmed that it was stupid, and
never did it again.*

Confronted with a choice, Sage decided to stick with his philosophy and do
what he thought was best. He says teens should "think for themselves."

A positive philosophy turns into a positive attitude, which turns into positive
actions, which lead to positive results. A negative philosophy does the opposite:
It produces a negative attitude, which produces negative actions, which lead to
negative results. Remember the ripple effect. It works both ways.

ACTION STEPS

- Have you ever been faced with a choice that went against
  your philosophy?
- What happened? Would you make the same choice now?

POINT #3: CHANGE YOURSELF BY CHANGING YOUR PHILOSOPHY

If you want to change what's happening in your life, change your
philosophy or *how you see things*. When you do that, you'll be able to take
the steps that will lead you to the answers you need. Changing how you
see things is not some huge task, but comes down to—you guessed it—
small steps.

Tamecka Crawford, 19, learned the power of changing her philosophy
when she went away to college. She lived in a foster-care group home and
was very scared and insecure:

> *How would I survive all alone in a strange place? Could I make it as a
> college student? Would I fail or drop out? I worried about people finding out
> I lived in a group home and treating me differently or making fun of me.
> I even wondered if my professors would treat me differently.*
>
> *When I first started classes, things seemed fine. But after a little while
> I met a guy and started spending lots of time with him, skipping classes*

and not studying. I felt I had all the time in the world to pull my grades up. So I started missing classes and my grades dropped tremendously.

I found myself using the excuse of being in foster care every time I missed a class or failed an exam. A lot of times I would say to myself, "Oh, I live in a group home. Who cares if I go to class or not?" I felt as if the words group home child were hanging over my head. Even though nobody treated me differently, in the back of my mind I felt they were.

My self-esteem was very low. I just gave up and didn't care. As a result, I completed my first semester with a 1.0 grade point average (like a D average), and ended up on academic probation during my second semester.

I felt nobody cared for me. I didn't have any family support. I kept making the mistake of comparing my life to students who had parents calling and visiting them. The other students would get care packages filled with all sorts of things, including their favorite foods, money, and supplies they asked for. I wanted so badly to have someone care about me like that. I felt neglected, not to mention jealous.

I remember hearing my roommate talk on the phone with her mother, describing her day and what classes she liked. I wished so badly that could be my mother or somebody who really cared for me.

But gradually, Tamecka's attitude changed:

If you want to change what's happening in your life, change how you see things. Changing how you see things is not some huge task, but comes down to taking small steps.

Just before the end of the first semester I realized I was wasting time feeling sorry for myself and had to do something about it. I never thought the semester would go by so quickly. When you first get to college you think you have all this time, and then before you know it, it's over. I realized that I was so wrapped up in worrying about having people do things for me that

I wasn't taking the time to care for myself. I got tired of using foster care as an excuse. I was tired of failing my exams. I was tired of crying. I noticed the people I was envying weren't doing so well in their classes, either. I finally realized it wasn't because I was in foster care that I was failing my classes. It was because I had been paying too little attention to my schoolwork. It wasn't being in a group home holding me back—it was me holding myself back.

By looking deeply at the way she saw herself, Tamecka realized that she needed to change her philosophy.

I had to accept the fact that I was in foster care and move on. Right after spring break I decided to wipe my eyes and find ways to start my independent life. I decided to attend all my classes and start pulling my grades up. I began studying night and day, especially subjects like history, which I always had problems with. I got help from peer tutors (fellow college students who were good in a particular subject). In exchange, I'd type a paper for them or make them dinner. I started letting professors know I was having problems and met with them to get help.

My next step was to see a therapist. I'd had counseling in the group home, but I never liked it because I felt we were prejudged. But in college I realized I needed help dealing with the transition from group home to college life. I talked about school, foster care, and other things on my mind. At the end of the sessions, she gave me suggestions about how to deal with my problems. It helped me realize that while I couldn't have the family relationships that I wanted so badly, I could thank God for the people who were taking the time out to help me any way they could.

I also got a part-time job to make some extra money. I was even able to put some money in the bank for rainy days. Basically, I started to depend more on myself.

Through counseling, I realized that people aren't better than me just because they live with their biological families. I also realized that, in some ways, being a foster child was an advantage. For example, I had already learned how to live with different people's personalities and attitudes. And I already had a sense of independence.

Yes, I still felt envious. When other students were planning their spring breaks in Hawaii or Virginia, I was deciding on what movie I was going to see. Sometimes I would end up staying at the group home for the whole vacation. But I pulled up my grade point average to 3.0, which was great compared to how things were looking at the end of my first semester.

Tamecka didn't ignore her problems or pretend they didn't exist. Her problems were real. Not having parents to support and guide you is real. Fear of failure in college is real. Being envious of people who seem to have more than you is real.

But when Tamecka changed her philosophy, she changed her life. She didn't completely forget her circumstances, but accepted them and then used them to her advantage. She put her focus on the only time that matters—the present, or what she could do in the moment to improve her situation.

One of the quickest paths to success is to get out of the past. Sure, it's smart to review mistakes and unhappy events because that helps you to make better choices in the future. Review, understand, and take responsibility for the errors you've made. (And don't spend a great deal of time doing even that!) Then use the past as a tool to do things differently in the present and move on.

ACTION STEPS

- Do you tend to get stuck in the past?
- What can you do in the present to create the future you want?

Sometimes it's not necessary to completely change your philosophy. Instead, you can use the philosophy you already have in a new way that works better for you. That's what Tonya Groover did.

Tonya was always outspoken in high school—in the wrong ways.

I was not the straight-A student. I was fighting all the time or getting into confrontations. I'd sometimes talk back to the teacher.

She did better in school when she started using her outspokenness in a new way—to ask challenging questions rather than confront people.

> *I'm not afraid to ask questions. For example, how did Christopher Columbus discover America in 1492 if the Native Americans were already living here? Let's be real about this. Those are the types of questions I would ask. You have to use your attitude to your benefit. You have to know when to use your attitude and when not to use it.*

Tonya is now a graduate student studying to get her Ph.D.

ACTION STEPS
- What are the most positive parts of your philosophy?
- How could you use those positive parts in better ways?

POINT #4: WHAT YOU THINK MATTERS, TOO

What you do matters. But what you think and say to yourself matter, too. Perhaps even more, because what you think determines the source of your attitudes (your philosophy).

More than a hundred years ago, in a book called *As a Man Thinketh,* James Allen explained that the single most powerful factor in determining the course of your life is not your circumstances (what happens to you), but the way you think. Here is what Allen wrote:

> *The mind is the master weaver, both of the inner garment of character and the outer garment of circumstance.*

In other words, what you think determines who you are and what happens to you. Your thoughts have the power to determine how you see yourself, other people, and the world. Your thoughts have the power to determine your actions, behavior, and how others respond to you. Your thoughts are directly linked to the type of person you become.

This is true of positive thoughts. And it is also true of negative thoughts.

When Tamecka told herself she couldn't do well in college, guess what happened? When she changed her philosophy—when she told herself she could take action to do well in college—her entire experience changed.

Look at what she told herself when she first got to college:

- I'm different from everyone else.
- People judge me because I'm in foster care.
- No one cares whether I go to classes or fail.
- Everyone else is happier and doesn't have problems.
- I don't have a chance of doing well in college.
- I can't do well in college because I don't have family to support me.

Now compare it with the new things she started telling herself:

- I have the ability to pay less attention to my boyfriend.
- I have the ability to attend classes and study hard.
- I can get help from peer tutors.
- I can get help from my professors.
- I can get help from a therapist.
- My foster care experience wasn't completely negative but a source of strength.
- Other students don't have perfect situations.
- I'll have bad days, but I can get through them, by using my own resources and help from others.

For Tamecka, it came down to a simple but incredibly important realization:

It wasn't because I was in foster care that I was failing my classes. It was because I had been paying too little attention to my schoolwork. It wasn't being in a group home holding me back—it was me holding myself back.

We're always talking to ourselves, but most of the time we're not aware of what we're saying or how it affects us. And there is no more powerful voice than that silent voice in our minds.

HOW THE BRAIN WORKS

To understand why thinking is so powerful, let's take a quick detour through your brain.

Your brain has both conscious and unconscious functions, and it's important to understand the difference.

Your conscious brain is the part that does the "thinking." It focuses intensely on one thing at a time, like a flashlight beam scanning a dark room. The conscious brain is incredibly powerful at what it does, but its scope is very limited. For example, you can't remember more than a few numbers in your head at one time. Prove this to yourself: Open the phone book, read three phone numbers at random, close the book, and see if you can remember even one of them.

But your unconscious? It can remember lots of information at the same time! If your conscious brain is like a flashlight, shining on one object at a time, your subconscious brain is like a floodlight that lights up everything at once—but only on a subconscious level (which means you're not aware of it).

Your conscious brain is easily distracted. The average person loses focus six to 10 times per minute (you know that from being in school). How often does your subconscious lose focus? Try never.

That's the key that most people don't realize. We think of our conscious functions—our will, our conscious decisions, our conscious thoughts—as what is really "us," and our subconscious as something that's going on under the surface and not so important. The truth is, the subconscious runs virtually everything.

And that's why some people end up in negative situations or living the life they don't want. They say to themselves, "How did I get here?!" They got there on automatic pilot—their actions programmed them into the life they ended up with. They weren't *conscious* of their choices.

So, how do you program your life? How do you help your subconscious make the right choices and decisions? In the same way you learned to walk or tie your shoes or skateboard: by taking small, positive steps over and over, until your actions are handed off to your subconscious. Then you can take those steps without thinking.

Because at that point, they've become a habit.

You know the expression, "Be careful what you wish for—you just might get it"? It's not even a question of what you wish for: Be careful what you *think*. Because what you think, multiplied over time, will create what you get.

This may be hard to believe, but it's the truth. Your "dominant thoughts"—the thoughts you have so often that they become habits of thought, or the automatic responses of your mind—do in fact determine what you will do in life. Whatever circumstances you encounter in life (and we don't have much control over what life brings), it's the way you *think about those circumstances* that will determine how you respond to them. And how you respond determines your actions and the path you take.

Remember, you are the most influential person in your life. There is nobody more effective at supporting your success—and nobody more effective at undermining it.

Think about this from your own experience. No two people react to the same situation in the same way. We've seen that from the teens in this book. Ferentz made the most of his talents while his friends did not. Octavia dealt in positive ways with her depression after going into foster care. Jordan kept plugging away as she tried to start a theater company at age 10. These teens were successful because of the ways they thought, because of the things they told themselves.

As Sir Edmund Hillary, the first man to climb Mount Everest, put it:

It is not the mountain we conquer, but ourselves.

You can look at anything you do, and by the message you give yourself about it—by the way you think about it—turn it into a success or a defeat. You can turn failure into success, and you can turn success into failure, by the sheer power of what you tell yourself.

Here's an example. You fail a test in school. What do you say to yourself?

▸ "It's the teacher's fault for making it too hard."
▸ "The school system shouldn't require all these tests."
▸ "I didn't have time to study for it."
▸ "I did my best and will try to do better the next time."

- "I'm going to study the questions I got wrong and do more homework in those areas, so I can do better the next time."

Quite a difference between these statements, right? Did you also *feel* a difference as you read them? Telling yourself negative things will certainly make you feel (and act) differently than if you tell yourself positive things.

Here's another example. Think back to a time you did something well that was really hard to do. What did you say to yourself?

- "I have the skills to do that again."
- "I was lucky and that was just a fluke."

In other words, did you put yourself down or give yourself credit? Did you see your success as something you achieved through your talent and skill, or as an accident?

How you talk to yourself determines how you view what happens to you—good or bad—and how you will respond in the future.

When Jordan was starting her theater company, she remembers having a lot of doubts, but she didn't give up.

> *I couldn't drive myself places, I couldn't sign contracts, I couldn't really do a lot on my own. I was just a little kid. But don't be afraid of the word no. Most of the time you'll have 10 to 15 no's before you get that one yes that will get you to your overall goal.*

Dallas Crilley was only 15 when he wrote a book about teens who started their own businesses. He accomplished this goal because he thought in positive ways.

> *If attitude isn't everything, it's close to everything. There's always a way to reframe the way that you're thinking. If you got a bad grade on a test, you can reframe it to, oh, well, what can I learn from this? The problem with attitudes is that once you have a negative attitude, you get used to being in that attitude. It gets kind of hard to fall into a more positive attitude. You want to get into the habit of thinking positively and then eventually it will come naturally.*

Dallas uses an important word—*reframing.* It means changing the way you think about something, to have a more positive result.

Kyle Freas often felt discouraged when he was trying to raise money to help abused children. But he learned to deal with setbacks and rejection and kept going.

> *Perseverance is a cliché but it's pretty huge. Lots of times I've been turned down, or I e-mailed someone about doing a project and heard no word back. I try not to get discouraged about that. I'd have to approach teachers and student councils, and sometimes they would be responsive and sometimes they wouldn't. Sometimes a charity or a foundation would respond, and sometimes they wouldn't. Sometimes people act a little skeptical of me. When you're my age in high school, you say to yourself, "No one's responding, so why am I even trying?" It's discouraging and you don't even feel like trying, but you need to learn from your mistakes and approach things in a different way.*

Ralph Waldo Emerson described this truth of human nature accurately:

> *Men succeed when they realize that their failures are the preparation for their victories.*

No one has more influence over you than you do. Nobody gets into your head more than you do, and there are no messages more powerful than the ones you tell yourself.

Other people may doubt your dreams and do their best to pull you off your path. You know people like that—people who can disappoint you and hurt you. But other people don't have the power to stop you because they don't have the power to control your most important tool—your attitude and the way you think.

ACTION STEPS
- Are your thoughts mostly positive or negative?
- How can you change what you say to yourself?

Think About It

What's Your Philosophy?

If you could sum up in a few sentences how you see yourself and the world, what would you say?

✎ Are you pleased with the way you see yourself? Are there things you want to change?

✎ What about the way you see the world? Is it a welcoming place or a scary one? Or neither?

However you see it, write it down below.

Here's how I see myself:

_____

_____

_____

_____

_____

_____

And here's how I see the world:

_____

_____

_____

_____

_____

_____

_____

Now, think about what you just wrote. Why do you think you see your-self and the world that way? Where did your philosophy come from? Write your thoughts below.

_____

_____

_____

_____

_____

_____

_____

_____

Are you pleased with what you wrote? Surprised? Saddened? Anything you'd like to change? Write your reactions below.

_____

_____

_____

_____

_____

_____

_____

_____

Maybe you're happy with what you've written. Maybe not. If not, that's OK—at least you know what needs to be changed. Whatever your philoso-phy looks like, the key to getting what you want, to creating your dream life, is to make your philosophy work for you and not against you.

If You Want to Change Your Life, Change Your Philosophy

But before you can use your philosophy to your full advantage, you have to know what parts of it are working for you and which parts are holding you back. Let's find out.

Before, on pages 32–33, you described your way of looking at yourself and the world. Look back at your answers. Now, think more deeply about what you wrote. What parts of your philosophy are helping you achieve success? Jot down your answer below.

_____

_____

_____

_____

_____

_____

Now, think about what parts of your philosophy don't work so well. Are there ways of seeing the world or yourself that are holding you back or causing problems in your life? Write your answer below.

_____

_____

_____

_____

_____

_____

Hold onto your answers for now. We'll be looking at them again.

How Do You Talk to Yourself?

How you think has a big effect on how you live your life. Try to remember a time when you were successful at something that was new or really hard. What did you say to yourself after you accomplished it? Whatever it was, try to remember it and jot it down here:

_____

_____

_____

_____

_____

_____

_____

Now, think back to a time when you tried to do something really hard and didn't do well. Can you remember what you told yourself? Write it down here:

_____

_____

_____

_____

_____

_____

_____

Did you give yourself credit for succeeding and believe you could do it again? Or were you very hard on yourself and not confident about succeeding?

Now think about your philosophy and the way you think. Then answer these questions.

How are your philosophy and the way you think related to each other?

_____

_____

_____

_____

_____

Are your philosophy and way of thinking mostly positive or negative?
For example, do you expect the worst or best from people? Do you tend
to put yourself down?

_____

_____

_____

_____

_____

How would you like to change your philosophy and the way you think?

_____

_____

_____

_____

_____

Use the Moment

U sing the moment means taking control of your life in the moment—right now, today. It means not blaming the past or worrying about the future. The only time you have is the present, because the past is gone and the future hasn't happened yet.

This can be a simple idea to understand, but a hard one to live by.

A lot of the past goes into who you are and what your life looks like—your parents, your childhood, your neighborhood, and your community. There's also your race and ethnic background. Let's not forget your school, your teachers, and your friends—and maybe some people who aren't your friends. And you're getting all sorts of messages from TV, movies, the news, and the world around you.

All of this is called your "circumstances" or your situation. And sometimes your circumstances can weigh pretty heavily on you.

It's easy to get caught up in your circumstances—the problems of right now. There's so much on your plate. You may feel like there are too many problems you don't have answers for and challenges you have no idea how to handle.

But guess what? The teens in this book say that circumstances may be affecting you, even driving you crazy, but they aren't who you are. And they don't determine who you will someday be.

POINT #1: YOUR CIRCUMSTANCES AREN'T YOU

Always remember this: Even with all your problems, there is still an *invisible you*. The invisible you is who you will be someday. Maybe not tomorrow or next week, but someday. And the little choices you make every day are what will put you on the path that takes you there. Whether or not you're aware of it, the little things you do every day—or don't do—are creating that invisible you of the future.

"Circumstances are a factor in what you become," says Tonya Groover, "but *you* are a factor in what you become. And that is more important."

Tonya grew up in a working-class neighborhood in Pittsburgh where a lot of people took the wrong path. But thanks to the choices she made back in high school to get back on the right track, she's now a graduate student.

> One reason I think I'm more successful than other kids my age is because I didn't let my circumstances make me. I was aware of problems in my community, and I made up my mind that I wasn't going to become a statistic. I made up my mind I wasn't going to be in jail. I wasn't going to have a baby before I got married. I was going to finish high school, go to college, get my Ph.D., and become an active leader in my community. And I wasn't going to let anything stand in my way.

Kyle Freas, 19, says it's important to learn from your past experiences, even your negative ones, but there's a difference between learning from them and getting bogged down in them.

Your present circumstances may be affecting you, but they aren't who you are. And they don't determine what you will someday be. There is still an invisible you, the person you will be someday—maybe not tomorrow or next week, but someday.

> It's natural to linger in the past about some things, and everyone should do that a little bit because you definitely have to learn through mistakes in life. You have to have bad experiences, because you'll never learn if you don't. But you're not going to be stuck in a situation forever. You can always climb out of it.
>
> I used to worry about the future and how things would be. But you can't control it. You can only prepare for it the best way you can. You need to live in the moment because the moment is the only thing you can live in. And try to take steps that will be good for your future.

And says Jacob Suarez:

> *The past is the past. It has made you what you are today. But if you don't take advantage of what is happening now, you're not going to have that bright future.*

ACTION STEPS

- How do you feel about your current situation?
- Do you feel happy with it or stuck in it?
- What would make you feel less stuck?

POINT #2: YOU CAN'T CONTROL WHAT HAPPENS TO YOU, ONLY YOUR REACTIONS

The problem with circumstances—the reason you can get bogged down in them—is that they're always changing. Bad things can happen to everyone, at any time. Life isn't fair. Some kids are poor, some live with only one parent, and some end up in foster care. One day it's bright and sunny, and you can't imagine life will ever get dark again. But then the next day something bad happens, and you can't believe life will ever get better.

Most of the crummy things that happen to us are *completely out of our control.* Just because we want the weather to be bright and warm doesn't mean that it will be. We can't control the weather, and we can't control our circumstances. We can gripe and complain, but we can't really do much about whether or not difficult times happen. They will happen. What matters most is what you do about the difficult times when they do happen. What you can control is how you feel about your circumstances. You can control how you feel about yourself. And you can control what you *do* about your circumstances.

How you view your circumstances makes all the difference between success and failure.

And that is *completely* within your control.

For Kyle, that kind of control means this:

Paying attention to how you influence people and not to how they influence you. When I was younger, I had the mentality of looking at how people influenced me, not the reverse. It's much better now that I see myself as an "influencer" rather than the one being influenced.

> You can't control your circumstances. What you can control is how you react to your circumstances and how you feel about yourself.

Tonya Groover talks about the difference between *reacting* to circumstances, which means getting bogged down in anger or blame or giving up, and *acting* to try to change them.

Are you going to be the person reacting, or are you going to be the person acting? It's better to be the person acting, because when you're acting and creating action, you're creating opportunities. You're creating outcomes and possibilities. But when you're always reacting to situations, circumstances, and consequences, then you're not going to get very far in life.

Although you may grow up in poverty and not have what other students your age have, or though your parents may not be able to throw you that Sweet 16 birthday party, you can make up your mind to throw that Sweet 16 birthday party for your kids. You can create opportunities for your children that you didn't have.

Why is it so important to act rather than react? Reacting usually means complaining or blaming. *Why did that happen? Why me? It's my parents' fault or my friend's fault.*

Taking action means taking control of what you can do to change your situation. And you can only take action in the present—not in the past, which is gone, and not in the future, because it hasn't happened yet. You can only create the future in the present.

Pauline Gordon, 20, knows the difference between reacting and acting. She's now in college studying to be a social worker. But, to get there, she overcame a lot of tough times as a teenager. She grew up in a housing project in one of the poorest and most dangerous neighborhoods in New York City. (One day when she came home, she found a bullet hole in her front door.) Actually, it's probably better to say that she *used* her past to her advantage instead of overcoming it.

I chose to do well in school because I always felt I had something to prove. I felt I was looked down on because I was the youngest child in my family. Both my parents are mentally ill. So I really felt like an outcast because of that. I always felt like I had to prove something to my family and friends.

Also, my sister was diagnosed with bipolar illness. She's another reason I try to do well. I want her to look at me as a role model, so she can do well too.

The strongest kids I know are not hindered by the experiences they've gone through. They've turned poison into medicine. I guess that's the term for it. They're making the best out of bad situations, and I would call that success.

Pauline has taken control of her future by acting in the present. By taking advantage of scholarships and financial aid, and by managing her money carefully, she's saved about $20,000 in the last year and a half.

After I graduated from high school, I started saving, saving, and saving. Whenever they had free classes about budgeting, saving, or banking, I went. I started researching banks that offered high interest rates on savings accounts, money market accounts, and certificates of deposit. I've been managing my accounts online. I even read some personal-finance books.

Pauline understands that taking small, positive steps in the present can have a huge impact on the future—even the distant future. Several months ago she opened her own retirement account, not something most teens and many adults think about. But the earlier

Reacting usually means complaining or blaming. Taking action means taking control of what you can do to change your situation. And you can only take action in the present—not in the past, which is gone, and not in the future, because it hasn't happened yet.

you start, the more money you'll have when you're older. Pauline found out it was easier to open an account than she thought.

> *You don't need a whole bunch of money to start a retirement account. You need to do your research. I got to start my retirement account with just $1,000. I'm pretty sure you can start one with even less, if you just do the research.*

Pauline could have gotten stuck in the poverty of her past, but she used the present to make a better future.

The sun is going to rise every day and keep rising for the rest of your life. And some days that sun is going to be hidden by dark clouds. But the "sun" of your own internal weather is something you can always control. That sun is your *intention*—what you plan to do.

You are not at the mercy of your situation or self-image: You get to create it. Yes, there may be days when it's cloudy and rainy. There may even be a tornado passing through. But you're in charge of your internal sun, and, if you choose, that light can penetrate a gloomy day and shine through.

Remember these two points.

- Self-esteem (feeling good about yourself) is not something you're born with or that you automatically either have or don't have—it's something *you create.*
- And you *can* create it. Right now, right in the moment. Your self-image, your view of yourself and who you are is something you build every day.

ACTION STEPS

- Do you feel you create your circumstances or your circumstances create you?
- Why do you feel that way?
- What could you do to change the way you see your circumstances?

POINT #3: WHEN YOU STOP BLAMING, YOU TAKE BACK YOUR POWER

When problems happen—when you're hurt, depressed, or angry—it's easy to blame other people. It's especially easy to blame them when they did something to deserve it! But when you grasp how the slight edge really operates in your life, something interesting happens:

You stop blaming.

When you stop blaming, you accept the fundamental truth that you are the *cause* of what happens in your life. You can then look at everything that brought you to this point—your parents, teachers, childhood, neighborhood, God, you name it—with appreciation and without blame. And what comes next in your life is your call.

You're free. The past isn't gone, but you have a different attitude toward it. Problems will still come your way, but you don't look at them in the same way.

Teens who are successful tend to take responsibility for who they are, where they are, and everything that happens to them. Taking responsibility for what happens to you—even when it hurts, even when it isn't fair is one of the most liberating things you can do.

When Tonya Groover was a teenager, she fell into the habit of making negative choices. Starting in seventh grade and throughout most of high school, she was in a clique of about 10 girls.

> In the neighborhood where I was growing up, everyone was in a clique. In high school we got into fights over who was cuter than who, or who had the hottest boyfriend. Eventually these confrontations became physical. And when it becomes physical, you're dealing with a situation where you could go to jail, get expelled from school, or lose your life. You can get killed if someone hits you in the temple or if someone has a pocketknife.
>
> I think one day I came to the decision that I wasn't going to fight someone else's battles. I had my own battles to fight. Most of the girls I had confrontations with, in my mind they weren't going to be anything. Why would I even waste my energy by battling or arguing with these girls? This came to a head when I was in 10th grade. I had to think about Tonya first. I wasn't going to

risk my life for someone else. It may seem extreme when I say I was risking my life, but that's what it is.

Tonya also understood the importance of time—that the actions she took as a young person would, over time, affect the rest of her life.

> *Your life starts in high school. The students who are focused in high school have it a lot easier, because high school is easier compared to college and graduate school. If you do good in high school, you can get a scholarship and you don't have to worry about financial problems in college. The more time you spend studying, the better your grades. The better the grades, the better the job. It's a domino effect that starts in high school.*

Tonya broke away from the clique. She didn't abandon her friends. She still stayed close with the girls but she set limits—she refused to participate in the negative things they did. Instead of blaming the clique or her circumstances for her behavior, she changed her behavior. Now 22, Tonya is a graduate student at a college in Pennsylvania, working toward her Ph.D. in computer science. She took actions that put time on her side.

Here's the problem with blame: When you don't see yourself as being the cause, when you react to crummy circumstances or events by blaming other people, the system, fate, or anything else, you are giving away your power.

On the other hand, when you take full responsibility—even when others are wrong or the situation is downright unfair and you really have been dumped on—you keep your life's reins in your own hands. Even when life is unfair.

Think about your friends for a moment. Do you know people who are always angry about what happened to them? How someone cheated them or treated them badly? Are they always complaining about what a jerk their ex-boyfriend or ex-girlfriend is? Or how unfair their math teacher was last semester for giving them a bad grade? Or how mean their friends were last year?

You might notice two things about this kind of conversation: 1) It's usually about blame and 2) it's usually about things that happened in the past.

But when you stop blaming your viewpoint shifts, from seeing circumstances as things that happen *to you*, to seeing circumstances as something *that you create*. You realize you're responsible for your life. And you also realize that your only limits are those that you—and not other people—put on yourself.

You have the power to choose those simple actions that will serve and empower you—and to keep on choosing them. And that slight edge moment happens every day, every hour, and every moment of your life.

ACTION STEPS
- Do you have the habit of blaming?
- What could you do to give it up?

POINT #4: SOMEDAY NEVER COMES

Let's hear it one more time: You can't change the past. You *can* change the future. And the only place you can change the future is now. You can think about the future, you can plan for the future, but you can't take action in the future. You can only take action now. Give up the idea of taking action "someday."

- Someday, when I feel more confident…
- Someday, when I feel good about myself…
- Someday, when I'm older and living on my own…
- Someday, when I have the time…
- Someday, when I have the money…

If you've ever said these things to yourself, there's some bad news: "Someday" does not exist. It never has and never will. There is no "someday." There's only today. Right now. This moment. When tomorrow comes, it will simply be another today; so will the next day, and the next, and the next. There is never anything but today.

And if you don't take action today, you're cheating yourself. Because your todays are limited. None of us has unlimited time. That might be hard to understand when you're 13 or 16 or 19, but it's true. That is what 16-year-old Kesly Coba learned. A few years back, she was extremely shy and quiet.

I remember sitting in class and feeling out of place. I would never partici-
pate. I was so shy that I didn't want to raise my hand to answer a question,
even if I knew that my answer was right. I always used to search the room
for girls with big hair so I could hide behind them. There was even a time
when a teacher gave me the wrong test grade, but I never complained. My
shyness kept me from it.

Not only was I shy by nature, but I was also uncertain about my English
because I had just come to the United States from Colombia. I was afraid
that if I said something wrong, people would make fun of me. So I just kept
quiet in order to not be ridiculed. My shyness was driving me so crazy that
I had become the "mute child"—until something unexpected happened to
shake me out of my skin.

On that day, Kesly and her family were driving to their cousin's bridal
shower. The family split into two cars, and Kesly rode with her cousins.

As normal kids, we demanded that the music be on full blast. I reached
down into my bag, pulled out my Snoop Doggy Dogg tape, and said "Hey,
play this! I'm sure everyone is going to like it." We all went crazy and
started rapping along, although I had no idea what Snoop was saying.

After about an hour, the first car pulled over to the side of the road and
then Kesly's car pulled over too.

As we stopped, I could see everyone running towards us with scared looks
on their faces, and I wondered what was wrong. "Get out of the car!" Luis
yelled, and I saw my mother crying in the background.

When we got out, smoke and flames surrounded our car. I saw a man
running towards us with a fire extinguisher, and that's when I started to
cry. I realized that our lives had been in danger.

As I sat on a nearby hill, I started thinking about what might have hap-
pened if the flames had gotten to us. I started to cry even more because I
realized that my dreams and expectations could all have ended that day.

This incident not only scared me to death, but also changed me for good.
After the accident, I started to open up and talk more. I didn't plan this,

but I guess that in my unconscious mind I realized that I had to change my shy ways, because being shy wouldn't get me anywhere. I realized God had given me a second shot in this world, so I decided to get the most out of it.

I started to raise my hand in class. At first I still felt nervous and too concerned about what others might think or say, but little by little I let go of my fears and just let the words pour out. My teachers and fellow classmates developed a new kind of respect for me, and I no longer felt boxed in by my shyness. My mother was very proud of me because she knew how ashamed I felt when the teacher used to ask a question and I was too shy to answer it.

It seems strange to have gotten such positive results out of a negative situation, but the truth is that scary or difficult experiences can make us think about what we want from life, and help us change and accomplish things we once viewed as impossible.

If you're waiting to start making changes tomorrow or the next day, remember this:

▸ You already have the skill, confidence, and strengths.
▸ You already have the time.
▸ You already have everything you need to achieve everything you want.

There's nothing to wait for. You can take action now.

ACTION STEPS
🗨 What are you waiting to do?
🗨 How can you stop waiting and take action?

Think About It

Past or Future?

Let's try an experiment to show you two different ways your mind works. Really do this—it's fun, pretty fascinating, and will take just a few minutes.

First, take a comfortable, seated position and look down at the floor, at a spot right between your toes. Take a few deep breaths, and then, staying in that position, take the next two minutes or so to think about your life. Anything and everything in your life—it doesn't matter what, just whatever comes to mind.

All right? Go.

What did you think about? Jot it down here.

_____

_____

_____

_____

_____

_____

_____

_____

Now, clear your mind, get up and walk around for a minute, then come back and do the second half of the experiment.

This time, take that same comfortable, seated position, only tilt your head up so that you're looking at the ceiling. Take a few deep breaths, and then think about your life over the next two minutes or so—again, it doesn't matter exactly what you think about, just focus on whatever comes to mind.

All set? Go.

What did you think about this time? Jot it down here.

_____

_____

_____

_____

_____

_____

_____

_____

Now, how did those two experiences compare? Did you think about pretty much the same things both times, or were they different?

For example, during the first part of the experiment, did you find yourself thinking about the past? Did any regrets come to mind? Did you find yourself thinking about things you could have or should have done differently?

During the second part, when you were looking up at the ceiling, did you find yourself thinking about the future? Were your thoughts and feelings more positive?

If so, you're not alone. Most people find it's pretty hard to not start thinking about the past when looking down. And when looking up, it's hard not to think forward into the future, about hopes, ambitions, and aspirations. It just seems to come naturally.

The point is this: Looking behind you will cause you to feel and act much differently than if you look to the future (and make plans to make it the best).

A Look in the Mirror

How do you view your present circumstances—your family, school, friends, neighborhood, and state of mind? What's going well? What's holding you back?

Think about each part of your life listed below. For each, do you tend to see yourself as at the mercy of what happens (not taking action), or someone who is in charge of what happens (ready to take action)? Be as honest as you can with this—and if you don't like any of your answers, don't worry: We're going to show you how to change them!

For Myself:

_____

_____

_____

_____

For My Friendships:

_____

_____

_____

_____

For My Health (physical, mental, and spiritual):

_____

_____

_____

_____

For My Wealth:

_____

_____

_____

_____

For My Education and Career:

_____

_____

_____

_____

For My Footprint on the World (what I want to accomplish or how I want to be remembered):

_____

_____

_____

_____

Perhaps this exercise helped you see where you need to take action. Lots of times we wait for a lucky break. But good things will happen if you start to take little steps to achieve your goals.

So let's start taking those steps....

Everything Starts with Small Steps

E very achievement, accomplishment, and success starts *somewhere*. Every task, large or small, begins with a first step. That first step can be hard to take. Yet one small step can lead to results you never imagined.

On a chilly day in December 1955, Rosa Parks was an unknown 42-year-old seamstress in Montgomery, Alabama. On that day she took a small step, because she decided she'd had enough. She was tired after a long day's work. Most of all, she was tired of being treated the way she was—and tired of every other person of her color being treated that way, too. So when she was told to give up her bus seat to a white passenger, she refused—even when the bus driver threatened her with arrest.

It wasn't an empty threat—Rosa Parks *was* arrested, convicted, and fined for violating a city law that black passengers had to give up their bus seats to white passengers. But the step she took led to the start of a new civil rights organization. Not long after, the newly formed Montgomery Improvement Association elected a young and relatively unknown minister named Dr. Martin Luther King, Jr. to be its spokesperson, launching a political movement that over the next decade ended legal segregation in the United States and transformed race relations in our country.

What difference can one step make? Think about Rosa Parks.

POINT #1: THE FIRST STEP LOOKS HARDER THAN IT IS

Yes, everything starts with a first step. But when you try something scary or new, taking the first step can look too hard. Some people get afraid and don't take that first step. But they don't chicken out because the first step is too hard—they chicken out because the first step *looks* like it's too hard. Who wants to make a mistake and look like an idiot, right?

Brian knows how hard the first step can look. He was afraid to approach a girl.

> *Some guys seem to find it easy to approach girls they don't know, but not me. The few times I've gone up to girls in the hallways at school or on the streets in my neighborhood, intending to get their phone numbers, I've given up at the last minute.*
>
> *One time I was chillin' at the bus stop with three friends. John spotted a girl coming our way. The guys and I stared at her as she walked down the street. Everything on her was looking good except the look on her face. She pointed her eyes to the sky, acting as if she were too busy for anyone.*
>
> *John said to me, "Yo, Brian, that girl looks like your type. She got on glasses just like you and she seems the nerdy type. Why don't you go up and talk to her?"*
>
> *I was afraid to talk to her because I didn't want to get rejected in front of my friends, and the girl's expression made it plain that that would happen. Besides, she was already halfway down the street, so I figured that I had missed my chance. But I thought to myself, "She is fine. If I ever see her again when I'm by myself, I'm gonna talk to her."*
>
> *A week later, I saw the same girl again at the bus stop, but this time I was alone. Since the guys weren't around, I thought, "This is my chance. There's nobody around to see me if I fail."*
>
> *Once again, she was walking mad fast and I had to hurry to catch up to her. I politely said, "Excuse me, I'd like to know your name." She rolled her eyes and started to ignore me. Then she asked, with a big chip on her shoulder, "Why do you wanna know?"*
>
> *I told her that I was interested in her. She replied, "I got a boyfriend already."*
>
> *That was the end of the conversation. I walked away from her because I wanted to save myself a little dignity (if I had any left). I felt like a total loser. I hoped I would never see her face again so I wouldn't be reminded of this horrible episode. I thought about how I wasted my time trying to talk to a girl who I knew would be stuck-up.*

But later that week I saw the incident in a new light. After I thought about it, I decided that what happened wasn't all that bad. At least I threw my fear aside and approached the girl.

Even after he got up the courage to take the first step, Brian still didn't get what he wanted. Or maybe he did—he faced his fears and, by taking that risk, perhaps it will be easier for him the next time and he'll do better. Brian was programming his subconscious—the more you do certain kinds of things (especially hard and scary things), the more you become comfortable with them, and the more they become a habit.

ACTION STEPS

- What first step are you afraid to take?
- What would help you take that first step?

POINT #2: THERE'S NO SUCH THING AS A LUCKY BREAK

Another reason people don't start taking small steps toward their goals is because they're waiting for a lucky break. Perhaps you know someone who's hoping to make the NBA or become a rap star.

The truth, of course, is that very few people have the talent to become superstars in sports or music, where the odds of making it big are a million to one. Everyone hoping to become the next Michael Jordan or Tupac will eventually find that out. And since the lucky break didn't turn out the way they hoped, they give up. They become victims of the lucky break myth.

A lot of people look up to the wrong role models for success. We make heroes out of people in sports and entertainment, but we don't see the years of hard work behind the success. Michael Jordan didn't become Michael Jordan overnight. Any great athlete pays the price: hours and hours and hours of practice with no one watching or cheering. Success in anything doesn't happen overnight or out of thin air.

Lucky breaks do happen—but not in the way you think. They are slowly grown, like a crop: planted, cultivated, and ultimately harvested. Success is not a random accident. Life is not a lottery.

Dallas Crilley, 15, knows this truth. He created his own big break when he was bored one summer. He saw opportunity where others didn't and took action.

I was sitting around doing a whole lot of nothing, and I knew that I wasn't the only one. All of my friends were doing the same exact thing—sleeping in, watching TV, and eating all three food groups: Cheetos, Ramen Noodles, and a whole lot of Coke. After a while, I started asking myself why. The theory that I came up with was that in our society, there seems to be this imaginary number of "18," and until you hit that age you can't make any money.

That didn't really make sense to me—when you're a kid, aren't those supposed to be your best dreaming years? The pressures of society haven't beaten down kids, so they have all of these hopes and aspirations. Why shouldn't kids be able to apply their creativity to the business world, since so many adults lose their creativity as they get older?

Dallas set out to look for kids who had ignored that rule and followed their dreams while they were still teens. What he found amazed him.

After a few Google searches for "kid entrepreneur" or "teen inventor," I found that there were tons of kids who had ran a successful business before 18! Knowing a good idea for a book when I saw one, I decided to stop kidding around and get writing.

So Dallas decided to write a book about kids who had run a successful business before they turned 18. He began by writing a chapter a week over the summer.

It was a great idea, but making a great idea into a reality always comes down to small steps. And those small steps can trip you up. At one point, Dallas found it hard to keep going.

About halfway through, it seemed there was still so much to do. It was hard to keep finding stories. But I set a time that I would write every day. Initially

it was a chapter a week. And I had to have that chapter a week. Even if it was Sunday and I was tired, I had to have another chapter written.

But eventually I started to learn to enjoy it. I started looking forward to these writing times. I'd turn on some music to kind of fit the vibe I was in, to get in the rhythm of writing.

The little steps fell into place after Dallas took the big first step:

I think getting yourself off the couch is the hardest part. And once you get a set schedule and a set method of doing things, and you keep doing it every day, it gets easier and easier from then on.

I don't think luck plays a role in success at all. If something good happens to you, in some way or another you did something that caused that to happen. I think waiting to get lucky is an excuse for laziness. You can't just buy a lottery ticket every day and convince yourself you're going to get rich. You have to take things into your own hands.

Waiting for a lucky break puts you at the mercy of the world around you. That's a pretty passive place to be. Over time, it creates a victim mentality, and that mentality tends to become a self-fulfilling prophecy. It keeps people from ever taking action and creating breaks for themselves. And the only way to create those breaks is through small steps—the power of simple daily actions, compounded over time.

ACTION STEPS

- Are you waiting for a lucky break to happen?
- Is there an opportunity you can take advantage of right now?

POINT #3: MAKE THE STEPS AS SMALL AS YOU CAN

When you find it hard to take steps toward a goal, the teens we talked with suggested that you break the task into the smallest possible steps. That way it won't look as scary. For example, if you want to write poetry, play a musical instrument, or learn a new language, you can start by doing it 10 minutes a day. Ten minutes a day of anything can have a huge impact on your life. If you start with small steps, you're more likely to stick with the task than avoid it.

Jacob Suarez used to love to put things off to the last minute.

> *I was a big procrastinator, like really big time. I'd have an eight-page paper due or something... and it would be the night before, and I'd be, "Uh oh, I got an eight-page paper due."*

Then he got a huge assignment—he had to design a theater production for a school project.

> *I had to choose the lighting and draw the sets to scale, I had to have a budget, I had to have costumes, I had to have a whole bunch of stuff. I had two months to do it for our final. What I did was make a schedule to break it down. I made a list of everything I needed to get done, and what day it needed to get done by. Essentially I created a deadline for each little thing. I would do a costume this day, a set design the next day. I'd write down all the things I needed.*
>
> *It seems like a daunting task at first to change your attitude and the little things here and there, but once you break it down it will make you so much more successful in the long run.*

By taking this huge project and breaking it up into small pieces, Jacob made it a lot less frightening and overwhelming.

Desiree Bailey, 19, is in her first year of college and uses very small steps to manage all her responsibilities.

> *Sometimes when I look at my schedule—a paper due, an exam on Tuesday—I'm thinking how the heck am I going to get everything done and make it through the week in one piece. It's really helpful to calm down, not stress out, and say, "OK, I can't get anything done at all if I sit here and think about everything I have to do." So I break it up—I say I'm going to do this on Monday, I'm going to do this on Tuesday, and then I can move onto the next thing. Maybe I can do half of a paper, depending on what's due first. It's so easy to get overwhelmed when you look at things as one big task.*

Chapter 4

ACTION STEPS
- Are you having trouble starting or finishing something because it seems too big?
- What's the smallest step you can take to get started?

POINT #4: THE SECOND STEP IS JUST AS IMPORTANT

The first step is key, but the second step is just as important. Lots of people take the first step, don't see any immediate success, and quit. How many people have the strength and courage to take the second step?

When you were an infant, you made your way around your world on your hands and knees crawling. Everyone around you was walking, and one day you got it into your little head that maybe you could give walking a try.

You grabbed onto something above you and pulled yourself upright. You stood up, holding onto that playpen, chair, or big stuffed animal. You were wobbly and unsure, but you were on your way, and there was no turning back. You let go and took that first, amazing, bold step—and *smack!* You fell right on your butt.

So what did you do? Did you think, "I hope nobody saw that. You know, maybe I'm not cut out for walking. And crawling isn't so bad. Lots of people crawl…"?

Of course not. You did what every other infant has done throughout time—you got back up and took a second step.

The second step was probably no better than your first. But that second step was where you really started to learn how to walk. From that point on, it was only a matter of time before you were really walking—no hands, no holding onto Mom or Dad, all by yourself. Every baby instinctively understands the slight edge. We forget it only as we grow up.

Alison, 17, knows a lot about the second step. When she was a junior in high school, she started to look for a job:

> Working in a clothing store was the first thing that occurred to me. I figured I'd get paid to hang out with guys while getting huge discounts on clothes. I asked in every store if they were hiring. I got really excited every time they told me to fill out an application. I figured that I would soon be picking and choosing from a lot of job offerings.
>
> But my "sure thing" turned out to be a ridiculous fantasy. I waited for the stores to call me back and they never did. I tried again a few months later and, once again, no calls came in. Eventually I lost interest in getting a job.

The first step failed. It would have been easy for Alison to give up, but she didn't.

> Then, last summer, I decided to look for an unpaid internship. Since I had worked on my school newspaper and was considering a career in journalism, I called every newspaper I could think of. I accepted the first offer I got from a community newspaper. (You'd be amazed at how easy it is to get a job when you're willing to work for free.)
>
> I worked two days a week doing the things no one else wanted to do, like typing other people's articles into the computer. But I also got to write a lot of little articles. I really enjoyed the work.
>
> At last I had real experience and a work reference (someone who could say I was a good worker). So in the beginning of my senior year, I started to look for a paying job again.
>
> I was smarter this time. When I went into a store, I'd introduce myself to the manager and find out exactly what they were looking for BEFORE I filled out the application. I began to carry around the information that I used to forget to bring with me, like the phone number and address of the person I was using as a reference. Most important of all, I always asked when I could call, rather than assuming that they would call me. I had a stack of business cards with the names and phone numbers of managers

I'd spoken to. Every day I would call to find out whether they'd made a decision. The hard part of all this was trying to be persistent without becoming a pain in the butt.

All my work (and good timing—stores were doing their Christmas hiring) paid off. I was offered not one, but three interviews—at Bloomingdale's, Barnes and Noble, and Express Ltd.

But my trials and tribulations were not over yet. Bloomingdale's put me through an intense screening process. I was interviewed three times. Next, I was supposed to attend a two-day training program on a Saturday and Sunday. Unfortunately, that Saturday happened to be the date of the SAT's. They wouldn't let me do it on another weekend, so I had to say, "Goodbye, Bloomies."

Then Barnes and Noble called and offered me the lowest of the low positions—cashier. The job was really easy, except that my feet were in the most pain I have ever felt. I wasn't used to standing on them for five or more hours at a shot.

I got my first paycheck after two weeks and it was HUGE. And the employee discount at Barnes and Noble was 30 percent off, which is really good, especially combined with a sale.

Success, right? Yes, but Alison was looking to take new steps to be even more successful:

The hourly pay was only $4.75, so I began looking around for bigger and better wages and discounts. I called Bloomingdale's again and found out that there was a position still available. Since the pay was $6 an hour, plus 15 percent off on almost anything in the world, I was out of Barnes and Noble within a few days and started a new job at Bloomies. Mostly I worked as a cashier, but occasionally I had to restock displays of merchandise.

I volunteered for overtime the next day (that's when you work more than your scheduled hours and get paid extra for it), which was a big mistake. I worked from 9 a.m. to 9 p.m. and almost died. I had an hour for lunch and a 20-minute break (better than Barnes and Noble, where I got a half hour lunch and a 15-minute break). The bad thing about Bloomies was that my

schedule changed every week. I was supposed to work 19 hours a week (three
evenings and a weekend day), but I always ended up working both weekend
days for a total of 22 to 24 hours.

But I didn't mind. I was having fun. Over Christmas vacation I did a lot of
overtime and was really raking in the bucks, because they paid time and a half
($9 in my case) for every hour that you worked over your scheduled hours.

ALISON WAS SUCCESSFUL BECAUSE:

- She adjusted her course. When she didn't get a paying job at first, she took an unpaid internship. That experience led to a paying job later on.

- She was persistent. Looking for a job is one of the hardest things in life, for anyone of any age, but Alison didn't give up.

- She started at the bottom. She took the first job offered to her, even if it was the lowest paid position in the company.

- She put up with difficulty on the job. Her feet were killing her, but she still showed up.

- She created her own luck. By not giving up and taking action, she put herself in the position to take advantage of a better job when it came around.

When you start something new, you feel excited. But then the excitement wears off and the new job or new relationship or new guitar isn't as exciting as it was before. This is the hard part of the journey—the long stretch between being a beginner and mastering a task. The middle part is when you need the most encouragement to stay on the path. No one was cheering for Alison when her feet hurt, during the middle part of her journey. Yet she made it through all the stages:

- **Beginning:** She was looking for a job, with no luck.
- **Middle:** She was dead tired, working hard, and her feet were killing her.
- **Mastery:** She was working overtime and making good money.

The middle of the journey is the easiest place to give up. But Alison stayed on the right path. It wasn't a question of luck or big breaks, but of putting one foot in front of the other. Little steps.

ACTION STEPS

- Have you ever been afraid to take a second step toward a goal?
- What could help you take it?

Think About It

The Power of Small Steps

Think about something you had to do in the past that seemed impossible—a project at school, saying sorry to a friend, participating in a sporting or outdoor event. It should be something that you thought you couldn't accomplish but did accomplish. Below, describe how you felt when you first thought about tackling this big thing in your life.

_____

_____

_____

_____

_____

_____

_____

Now, looking back, think about the small steps you took to tackle this challenge and how you felt afterwards. Describe those steps and feelings below:

_____

_____

_____

_____

_____

_____

After it was over, did the challenge seem as hard as it did at first? Did you get the confidence to tackle other hard challenges? Did you give yourself credit for succeeding?

A Single Step You Can Take

At the end of Chapter One on page 17, we asked you to describe three steps you could take in each area of your life to reach your goals. Now you can narrow it down even further—what is one simple thing you can do in the next 24 hours that would help you reach your goals in the following areas (just one thing):

Have fun with this—be creative!

For Myself:

_____

_____

_____

_____

For My Friendships:

_____

_____

_____

_____

For My Health (physical, mental, and spiritual):

_____

_____

_____

_____

For My Wealth:

_____

_____

_____

_____

_____

For My Education and Career:

_____

_____

_____

_____

_____

For My Footprint on the World (what I want to accomplish or how I want to be remembered):

_____

_____

_____

_____

_____

Hold on to your ideas. When we get to the last chapter, you'll start using them.

(But if you want to put them into action right now—go ahead!)

There's No Such Thing As Failure

By now you understand that the secret of success is failure. That's right—you have to fail in order to succeed. This can be a hard point to understand.

Thomas Watson Sr., a very successful businessman who founded the company IBM, once said this:

> *The formula for success is quite simple: Double your rate of failure.*

Double your rate of failure to be successful? It sounds a little crazy. Fail your way to success? When was the last time anyone told you to do that? The chances are probably never.

No, we don't get the message that failure can be a good thing. More likely, we try to avoid it at all costs. And why not? Who likes to fail?

As Desiree, 19, puts it:

> *Honestly, I'm one of those kids who's afraid of failure. And I realize it's something I have to come to terms with, because I realize it's necessary for personal growth and maturity. But at the same time, it's scary. It's very hard to see it as positive when you've failed.*
>
> *So many times I think I should have done this differently, or if I had only done that, but at the same time it's an opportunity to see how far you've come from that moment. And what you did wrong in the past can help you do something correctly or differently in the future.*

POINT #1: SUCCESS IS BUILT ON FAILURE

What looks like failure can be something else entirely. When Lucas Mann had his first date, it certainly appeared that he had failed completely.

My date and I had known each other since we were kids, but it had always been platonic. Then, about a month ago, I started to realize that I liked her as more than a buddy. I'd catch myself fading in and out when we talked because I was staring at her face. Man, that was stressful. I was killing myself over whether she felt the same way, whether I was going to ruin our friendship.

We decided to go to the movies, and when I picked her up I got up the courage to ask her, "Umm, do you maybe want to make this a real date?" She gave a shy smile and said, "Sure." I was momentarily overjoyed. But then my anxieties sprouted. Could people passing by tell I was nervous? Was my fly open? I kept glancing at her out of the corner of my eye, forgot to watch where I was going, and tripped over the uneven sidewalk.

"Slick," she said.

Cool. If I had to be a loser, at least I was a loser walking with a funny girl.

Finally we got to the movie and took a seat in the back row of the theater. The lights dimmed and I felt a familiar sensation—tickling in the nose, a sudden headache—that only meant one awful thing: an allergy attack.

The first sneeze was a monster. It exploded, forcing me to pull away to keep from splattering her. I excused myself and sprinted toward the bath-room. People gave me stares. My face was bright red, I was wheezing, and my eyes were watering.

In the bathroom I grabbed handfuls of paper towels and blew my nose for all it was worth. I took a bunch back to my seat. But there was no stopping the stream. I was sitting there with a river flowing out of my nose, making the sad noises of an asthmatic.

Of course, she was leaning back in her seat, more frightened by my leaking fluids than by the psycho on screen.

All seemed to be lost.

Walking home was a jumble of sneezing and panicked thoughts. All the things that went wrong were constantly replayed in my mind. We finally got to her house. There was the longest pause yet. I just stood there, thinking *over all the little things that happened. A quick hug and she was gone, the perfect end to an embarrassing night.*

Later, I had a hard time sleeping. The tripping, the allergy attack, the awkward silences. There would be no second date.

Still, the next day I forced myself out on a limb and called her. My palms were sweating as I prepared myself for rejection.

"Sooo, do you think, um," I stammered, "maybe you'd like to go out again?"

"Why not?" she said and laughed.

Amazing!

We went out to the movies again and this time it was a lot better. Let's just say that I can't tell you how that movie ended. We're still going out. It's only been a few weeks, but it seems to be going well.

So, there's a moral to this story: Just relax instead of thinking about every moment on your first date. Things can't possibly be as bad as the gruesome battle scene going on in your head.

Lucas got it right. Failure is in our heads. We create it. We interpret what happens to us. We put the labels on everything we do. We're the first ones to use the word *failure*—and usually about ourselves.

But how can you learn anything without failing at it first? Who ever does something right the first time (or the second, third, fourth, or fifth)? What if Lucas believed he was a failure and didn't ask for a second date?

ACTION STEPS

- Was there a time you thought you failed at something?
- How can you see it in a different way?

POINT #2: IT'S ALL IN OUR HEADS

Can you imagine if you'd been afraid of failure as a baby?

"Shoot, I knew I wasn't cut out for that whole walking thing. What was I thinking? I was crazy to even try!"

Teens who are successful know that falling down is the way you learn to fly. Tonya Groover doesn't believe failure even exists:

> I've failed classes in college, but when I go back to take those classes again, I already know the material and have gained a deeper understanding of it. I don't think there is such a thing as failure, because you always have a second chance. When you learn to ride a bike, you have to fall off a couple of times. When you fall down, you get back up. There's an expression—you have to go through something to get somewhere.
>
> If you talk to anyone who has a high position or anyone you look up to, nobody gave them everything so they can be where they are. Nobody's giving out jobs, nobody's giving out grades. Nobody's giving out anything. You've got to work for it. And when work is involved, there's also competition and failure. But that's okay, because eventually you know what kinds of things you're suited for and which things you're not.
>
> You have to fail a couple of times. But you shouldn't look at it as failure. Let's say you apply for a scholarship but you don't get it. Go back to the scholarship committee and ask them why you didn't get the scholarship. Did you need to improve the way you answered the questions? Was it your SAT scores? Were your grades not high enough? You can ask for constructive feedback. It's about critically analyzing yourself.

Whether or not you want it to happen, you're going to fail at one time or another. Everyone does. If you go through life with the philosophy that failure is bad, you'll be too hard on yourself when things don't go as planned. You'll never learn from your mistakes. You'll never grow as a person. You may be so afraid of failure that you won't even try in the first place.

To put it in perspective, consider the following:

▸ A young African-American woman wanted to work in TV and became the evening news anchor for WJZ-TV in Baltimore. But she was taken off the air because the station didn't think she was fit for television. She didn't give up, though, and kept giving TV a try. Her name? Oprah Winfrey.

▸ Bill Gates founded Microsoft and is one of the richest men in the world, but his first business venture was a flop.

▸ Michael Jordan missed more than 9,000 shots in his career and lost almost 300 games. Twenty-six times he missed the game-winning shot.

▸ If a baseball player hits .333 he's had a fantastic season. But it also means that he failed to get a hit almost 70 percent of the time.

▸ Thomas Edison, the inventor of the electric light bulb, tried out thousands of different versions of it and every single one failed before he invented the right one. His comment: "I have not failed. I've simply discovered ten thousand ways that don't work."

See if you can figure out who this is:

In 1831, he failed in business.
In 1832, he ran for the state legislature and was defeated.
In 1833, he failed in business again.
In 1834, he was elected to the state legislature.
In 1835, his sweetheart died.
In 1836, he had a nervous breakdown.
In 1838, he ran for speaker of the state legislature and was defeated.
In 1840, he ran for elector and was defeated.
In 1843, he ran for Congress and was defeated.
In 1846, he was elected to Congress.
In 1848, he ran for Congress again, and was defeated.
In 1855, he ran for Senate and was defeated.
In 1856, he ran for vice president and was defeated.
In 1858, he ran for Senate and was defeated.

Finally, in 1860, Abraham Lincoln ran for president of the United States—and won. Many historians now consider him to be the greatest American president. Think about that list you just read if you ever visit the Lincoln Memorial in Washington—if he had been afraid of failure, we never would have heard of him.

Here's another great example.

Back in the 1700s, a bishop named William Wilberforce was a member of the British Parliament. At that time slavery was legal in Britain and its colonies. Starting in 1788 and for the next 18 years in a row, Wilberforce introduced a bill in Parliament to end slavery. And every year, for 18 years in a row, his bill was defeated.

Finally, three days before Wilberforce's death in 1833, Parliament passed a bill to abolish slavery not only in England but also throughout its colonies. Not many years later the United States abolished slavery because Lincoln also refused to be afraid of failure.

Think of how history took a different path because of these two men. Think of how Wilberforce and Lincoln used failure rather than being defeated by it, and how the world today is better as a result.

What's true for great figures in history is also true for you.

ACTION STEPS

- Think about a time you learned from failing at something.
- What did you learn?
- How have you used what you learned?

POINT #3: FAILURE CREATES UNEXPECTED OPPORTUNITIES

Failure can help you discover positive parts of yourself you didn't know about and create new opportunities in your life that you never expected.

Jacob Suarez, 16, loves to sing and participates in school singing competitions. But one time he didn't win a competition and was very disappointed. He could have stopped singing, but didn't. Good thing he didn't.

I kept practicing and practicing, and it ended up that the girl who was supposed to go to the state competition wanted to do something else. So she dropped out and they asked me if I wanted to go in her place. And I went on to participate in the state singing competition.

When Kyle Freas was in elementary school, his teacher became frustrated with him. The teacher picked Kyle up and threw him hard against a chair. Kyle suffered injuries to his neck and became depressed. But something good came out of it.

> *It gave me a good perspective. It gave me sympathy for abused kids, because no one can understand what that situation is like until you're in it. Once you experience something like that, you can't imagine what it would be like for someone to be caught in that kind of situation all the time.*

Instead of making Kyle bitter, that incident is part of the reason why he became involved in raising money to help abused and critically ill children. Who knows? If Kyle had a better teacher and the incident never happened, perhaps he never would have developed as much sympathy for kids who need help.

Michelle Stallworth, 18, is another example of a teen who discovered her greatest strengths and talents only through failing. Michelle has to use a wheelchair because of an accident when she was a year old. When she was younger and her cousins asked her to play baseball or basketball, she always refused. She felt her braces and wheelchair made her look handicapped. But eventually a teacher encouraged her to give basketball a try and she started playing. Michelle loved the sport.

> *One day in the school lunchroom, I told someone that I hoped to play someday against really good wheelchair players in the Special Olympics. A girl overheard what I said and whispered to a guy, "Can you imagine a bunch of crippled people playing basketball?" The guy started acting like he was retarded and trying to dribble a ball. I didn't want anyone to know how hurt I was, so I didn't say anything. But after that I wanted to prove what a good player I could be.*

Michelle joined her high school's wheelchair basketball team. But in a game against a rival high school, things didn't go so well.

> *Throughout the game, my teammates would pass me the ball as soon as they got it, but the opposing players double- and triple-teamed me. I either lost the ball or threw up shots that hit nothing but the bottom of the hoop without going*

through. I missed an easy layup. I got fouled a couple of times but I missed all my free throws. I even got hit in the head by a pass.

I started getting really mad and screaming at my teammates. I started hogging the ball, but as soon as I did that, the coach called a time out and screamed at me. "Pass the ball! People are getting open!" So I went back in and passed to a teammate. He caught the pass but missed the shot. I just looked at the whole team with a vicious stare. We lost 33 to 12.

Michelle gave up.

After the game, I walked out on my team. I hated everyone on it. I thought they were all scrubs. The teachers who came to support us said I was a baby and a sore loser.

But then she had a change of heart.

It took me a while to calm down and finally admit that I was one of five people who had played horribly. I knew I needed to practice if I was going to improve my game so that nothing like that ever happened again. So I spent a lot of time during the summer playing with the walkers around my way. We played in the school gyms that were open and outside at the playground.

I also thought about playing on the street courts near where I lived, but I thought the guys would make fun of me. Finally I just decided to give it a try.

I went over to the court and a few guys were shooting around. At first things were a little scary and I was reluctant to join in. But I asked if I could play, and the guys said OK. I was the only wheelchair player on the court, but every time I would touch the ball they would tell me to shoot it, and that gave me confidence.

When one game was tied, a kid named Shawn said, "You're gonna get the last shot." He passed the ball to me when I got open under the basket. A defender was on me, but I shot the ball under his arms and it went in.

When school started again in the fall, all the practice paid off. Michelle's wheelchair team developed a better chemistry than they had the previous year.

They ended up playing in the city championships against the same team that destroyed them the year before.

> *Everyone was saying my team had no skills because of the way we played last year, so I came into the game thinking I had something to prove. During the first half, we got no respect. A scrub talked trash to me and made me so mad that I wasn't concentrating as well as I should have been. But the second half was a different story. I scored 18 points, had seven rebounds, seven assists, and seven steals. We beat them 29 to 17.*

Michelle was named Most Valuable Player.

> *For the next three days, I was the most conceited person you would ever want to meet. But then I realized it wasn't fair—my teammates had played great too. I told everybody who gave me credit that our win was a team effort. I'll always remember that game and the pizza party we had afterwards.*
>
> *I'm very thankful to basketball because it taught me how to make friends and not be so shy. I don't worry as much about people making fun of me because I'm in a wheelchair. Basketball also forced me to face some things about myself, from my quick temper to the fact that I'm a sore loser. I'm more in control of those things now.*

Think of how close Michelle came to never playing basketball again. If she had been defeated by her failure, she never would have become MVP.

Failure is just another word for hard or difficult moments in life. And life will hand us those moments, like it or not. Successful teens are not thrown off course by tough times. They have the ability to keep going even when they think they've failed.

ACTION STEPS
- Have you ever had an experience similar to Michelle's?
- What was it and how did it change you?

POINT #4: ANOTHER WORD FOR LEARNING

Mark Stumer, 18, learned that failure can be a great teacher when he and his friends tried to start a business in high school. And he learned that failing wasn't the end of the world.

> My friends and I had wanted to start a school store so we could make money. We had been selling lukewarm sodas from a little corner of the cafeteria, with three or four people chaotically giving out sodas and taking money.
>
> So when we got an assignment in business class to create our own business, we figured it was time to make our store a reality. At first we were going to sell only soda, but after a week or two of business, we merged with another group who sold candy and became a snack food juggernaut.
>
> To begin, we figured we at least needed a name. A few days later, a joke from The Simpsons gave us one: in one episode, Homer sings a little song about how he's so smart, but he misspells smart as "s-m-r-t" and accidentally sets the house on fire. It was so funny that we called the store SMRT (pronounced "smart"). We had an idea and we had a name. Now it was time to start learning how to make money.
>
> First, we had to decide what to sell. We went to a big chain store, armed with nothing but our wits and a calculator. We had to figure out which products could be sold for the biggest profit. We decided to buy candy that came in boxes of 200, and cost us 8 cents each. We sold them for $1 each. Every box cost us only $16, but earned us $200! That's a huge profit!
>
> Then we set up a table in the cafeteria with a wide variety of candy and cold sodas in coolers. We were doing steady business, pulling in between $200 and $300 a week. It was pretty cool selling behind the counter, but the hungry masses got impatient quickly, so it was also annoying.

Mark and his friends learned that running a business also has its downsides:

> Unfortunately, not every part of the company ran like clockwork. We hadn't put much thought into how we would use our profits. We decided that we would spend a portion of our profits to pay our senior dues. And if we made enough of a profit, each of us would receive a small amount of

cash. However, arguments about paying senior dues and how to split the extra money became constant issues.

"So, if we're gonna split the money, everyone should figure out how much money they deserve."

"Dan, you're an idiot! You think anyone's going to say, 'I'm not worth a share of the cash?' "

"Chill, dude. He's trying to get an idea of how to split the money."

"Everyone's gonna say they're worth so much, when some people aren't doing jack."

"Look, if this is how we're doing it, I'm worth like, 50 percent of the store. There're some people who never sell, don't come to meetings, or anything else, like…" I trailed off to avoid pointing fingers.

The fighting frustrated me. But I also learned a lot of lessons about running a successful business. The most important and obvious lesson is: Never, ever leave $300 in small bills lying around unguarded. (It got stolen.) That mistake was a definite setback. Everyone was upset that we lost half our money, and it caused several fights over whose fault it was.

Another big lesson is: When you go to restock your inventory, make sure the person with the chain store membership is with you! Forgetting this simple detail has complicated a few trips to restock and led to some fun arguments.

"Yo, Davina's comin' right?" I'd ask, since she was our member.

"No, her parents won't let her leave home."

"So, we have no card?"

"We might get Kristina's. She's supposed to call me at like 1 in the morning to let me know."

"And if we can't get it?"

"There's probably a way."

"You mean, I'm getting up at 9 A.M. tomorrow?" I'd sputter. "When we don't know if we're going?"

"Well… sorta."

A third, very important lesson is: Unless it's absolutely necessary, don't start a company with so many other people. We had nine people running one small store. With so many people, we were always having arguments. The *stress was finally too much, and we had to take drastic actions to save our friendships: One Friday in March, SMRT permanently closed for business.*

But even though the store folded, we learned a lot. Like how and why to use spreadsheets and databases, and how a vast number of careers depend on those basic skills. We learned how to (sort of) work together as a team for the greater good of the company.

And I've gotten a decent idea of what types of skills I'll need in the future, if I don't want to end up living in a basement apartment eating cold ravioli from a can.

Remember that in anything you do, you will experience failure. But no experience in life is wasted if you learn something from it. Failure is all in your mind, because the slight edge tells us that it's the only way to learn and grow.

ACTION STEPS

- After reading this chapter, do you have the same attitude toward failure?
- If you're still afraid of failure, what would help you change your attitude?

Think About It
The Key to Success Is Failure

Let's look at your own life. Think back to something you failed at (or thought you failed at). It could be a test in school, the first time you tried a new sport, or anything else you that didn't go as you expected. Describe what happened in the space below:

_____

_____

_____

_____

_____

_____

_____

Think for a moment about what you've written and answer this question: What did you learn from that experience? Did anything positive come out it, no matter how small? Write your answer below:

_____

_____

_____

_____

_____

_____

_____

Now ask yourself: What did I learn from this experience that I can use in the future? What can I do differently next time, either in the same situation or a different situation? Write it down below:

_____

_____

_____

_____

_____

_____

_____

Do you look at your "failure" in a different way? Do you see positive ways to use "failure" in the future? Jot down your thoughts:

_____

_____

_____

_____

_____

_____

_____

Chapter 6

Habits Are Powerful

- You know that little things matter.
- You know that whatever you accomplish, big or small, is made up of small steps.
- You know the power of acting now, in the present.
- You also know that failure is the greatest teacher you'll ever have.

Now it's time to talk about habits, the simple things you do over and over again, day after day.

We often take habits for granted. After all, they're habits—something you do without thinking. It's very easy to forget you have them.

POINT #1: HABITS RUN YOUR LIFE

But here's a secret about habits: They have enormous power. In fact, your habits are what run your life. Whether the habit is good or bad, you know that to be true.

A habit is simply an action that you have repeated and repeated until it becomes automatic. Your actions, repeated consistently over time, migrate from your conscious mind to your subconscious mind, and your subconscious mind is what really runs the show.

We've talked about the subconscious. It's a very powerful part of your life, although you're mostly unaware of it. You've learned to do certain things without thinking. In other words, you have passed control of your actions to your subconscious mind. That is, your actions have become habits.

Habits come out of your subconscious. When you put on your shoes, you don't think about it—you just do it automatically. Same thing when you ride a bike or brush your teeth—it's like you're on automatic pilot.

That's okay, if the habit is a good one. But what if it's not such a good one? What if you have a bad habit and you're not even aware of it?

Everyone knows about bad habits. You can fall into habits of thinking or speaking or behaving that are either positive or negative. Some people fall into cigarette habits or alcohol habits or drug habits. The focus of this chapter is not on bad habits, but on what you can do to develop good habits that will help you grow.

The good news is that your habits can be changed. And they can be changed if you understand where they're coming from. Habits are actions repeated over time—but do you remember where your actions come from?

your philosophy —> your attitudes
your attitudes —> your actions
your actions —> your life

Your habits are the result of the choices you make in the moment, which come from your thoughts, attitudes, and your philosophy—the way you see yourself and the world.

So once you're aware of a habit that doesn't serve you well, how do you change it or get rid of it?

The first thing to remember is that trying to get rid of an unwanted habit is a little like trying *not* to think about a pink elephant. The more you try to tell yourself not to think about the elephant, the more you think about it!

Why? When you put a lot of energy into focusing on what you *don't* want to do—by talking about it, thinking about it, complaining about it, or worrying about it—you usually get more of what you don't want.

Remember Tamecka? The more she thought about not doing well in college, the worse she did. Always remember the power of what you think about and focus on, perhaps the most

> Habits have enormous power. In fact, habits are what run your life. Whether the habit is good or bad, you know that to be true.

important habits of all. Because what you focus on, good or bad, grows. So it's better to develop the habit of focusing on what you *do* want.

This takes time—and it takes knowing where to focus your energy. The key to your success, to mastering your everyday habits of thought and action, is through changing your philosophy. And when you change your philosophy, you can change your habits and your life.

> When you put a lot of energy into focusing on what you don't want, you usually get more of it in your life. Because what you focus on, good or bad, grows. It's better to focus on the positive things you want, rather than the negative things you don't want.

Magda, 17, found out that it was better to focus on what she wanted rather than on what she didn't want or couldn't have.

> *For almost a year I had been desperately in love with Mike, and I thought that having him love me back was the purpose of my existence. Then my friend Anna started to spend time with him, and he fell for her. (By the way, I was the smart one who introduced them to each other.)*
>
> *I was very depressed. My self-esteem dropped as low as the temperature in Alaska. I spent whole days looking unsuccessfully for a meaning for my life. I was having pointless fights with my mom and I cried often, especially after Anna's calls about how happy she was with Mike. She thought I was over him, but the truth was they both hurt me.*

Being in love with Mike, and wanting Mike to love her back, was Magda's habit—a hard one to break. She got over it by starting new habits.

> *A year ago, I thought nothing in the world except Mike could help me feel better. I was wrong. I didn't realize that the world held many things that could heal my pain. To my surprise, the cure wasn't another guy to make me blush and sigh. I discovered that the key to saying good-bye to my depression was getting involved in new interests and activities.*

Cure #1: Helping Others

About a month after Anna and Mike got together, my friend Martin asked me if I knew anyone who would like to tutor an 8-year-old girl from Poland, the same country I'm from. "Yeah, me," I answered, only because I was looking for a way to earn money. The next day I met Kathy, my future student. She had been in the United States only a few weeks and needed somebody to teach her English. I agreed to come twice a week for two hours each time.

> Habits are tools that help you grow and develop as a person. Instead of serving your habits, make your habits serve you.

A week later, Martin found me two more customers, an 11-year-old boy and his 9-year-old sister. Spending 10 hours each week tutoring made me realize how rewarding it is to teach. When Kathy first started going to school here she couldn't understand anything. She felt lonely and sad. Now she loves school. Being the one who helped her made me feel really good.

Tutoring gave me a feeling of independence and improved my self-esteem. Furthermore, I enjoyed making my own money, and it was much more pleasant than sitting at home hopelessly wondering about that jerk going out with Anna.

Cure #2: Keeping Busy

Through school, I got involved in other activities that helped me get Mike off my mind. I got an internship at a kids' clothing company (internships are required at my high school) and also began volunteering at an animal shelter. Having a busy schedule helped my healing process. People at my internship helped me believe in myself because they appreciated my work, whether it was copying, filing, or proofreading.

My duties at the shelter—walking dogs, cleaning cats' cages, and feeding them—made me feel even more needed. I felt great and finally I was able to tell myself, "Life is not that bad." I didn't waste any more time wondering whether "he" would ever want to go out with me.

> *The other thing that made my summer great was that I did a lot of reading. I was looking for advice on finding someone special and keeping him, but the books helped me realize that I should not live for love and jump from the roof when I can't win somebody's affection.*
>
> *I realized that love is only one part of life. The incident with Mike taught me not to fall so hard for a guy and not to wait for him to like me. Now I give a guy a few weeks and if he doesn't show any signs, too bad for him. I move on.*
>
> *I am a junior in high school now, and I'm involved in a lot of activities that make my life exciting. In addition to working part time, I tutor, go to a gym and swim in the pool, read, study Spanish on my own, and, of course, go to school. I do all this during the week, so I have weekends free to see my friends. I feel I am more confident, independent, happy, and mature than I was a year ago.*

Instead of focusing on being with Mike, which wasn't going to happen, Magda put her focus on new interests and activities—new habits she could develop. She still feels sad sometimes, but now she tells herself she can overcome it.

ACTION STEPS

- Do you have habits you'd like to change?
- What new habits would you like to start? Why?

POINT #2: MAKE YOUR HABITS SERVE YOU

What limits you is never circumstance or fate. The limiting factor is always you and what you hold to be true in your mind. And if what you believe is positive, you'll have positive results. The wisest choice you can ever make is to believe in your unlimited possibility. And the tool you use to do that is habit.

There are two kinds of habits: those that help you grow, and those that hold you back. The first type of habit is a tool you can use to achieve success. The second type of habit makes you its slave—the habit doesn't serve you; instead, you serve it.

- Facing difficult feelings serves you well, while avoiding difficult feelings does not. By avoiding difficult feelings, it becomes harder to face them later on. Many people develop bad habits to avoid facing difficult feelings.
- Looking for the best in people serves you well. Expecting their worst doesn't.
- Looking for the positive side of every challenge can become a habit. So can finding a reason to complain.
- Putting a piece of every paycheck into a savings account can become a habit. So can spending more than you earn.
- Finding out what you believe serves you. Believing and accepting everything you read on the Internet or hear on television doesn't serve you.

Are you going to be a slave to bad habits? Or are you going to make your positive habits serve you?

ACTION STEPS

- Do you have a habit that helps you grow? What is it?
- Do you have a habit that holds you back? What is it?

POINT #3: TAKE SMALL STEPS TO DEVELOP GOOD HABITS

Lots of teens take small steps to replace bad habits with good ones. As you read their suggestions, think of how you can use them in your own life.

Tip: Develop a Schedule

Desiree Bailey used a schedule to develop the habit of doing her schoolwork:

I always did homework right after I came home. If you want to watch TV, tell yourself you're going to watch TV for an hour and after that you're going to do homework. You can take a break for a half hour, have a snack or something like that, but then go back to it. Having a schedule helps you get into the routine of using your mind.

Tip: Do Things Ahead of Time

Octavia Fugerson developed the habit of doing things ahead of time and seeking out opportunities, rather than waiting for good things to happen:

> When I was living at home, my mother didn't allow us to do homework. That was because I liked homework and she didn't like anything that I liked. My grades dropped and I failed three classes in the ninth grade. But at the same time I understood that if I was going to get somewhere, I was going to need my education. If I was going to get out of my situation, I wasn't going to get nowhere without an education.
>
> I tried to do my schoolwork ahead of time. I'd make sure I'd do it to retain the information, not just to pass. If I was struggling in class, I'd let the teacher know if I was having a really hard time with it. I'd try to get some extra help. I would go online and look for tutors. Online tutoring was the best for me.

Tip: Don't Get Down on Yourself

Don't get down on yourself if you've developed a bad habit. Almost everyone has one. Instead, see how you can adjust the habit into something better. Ralph Tarrant, 18, fell into the bad habit of wasting money before he took small steps to change that:

> It wasn't until I hit 18 that I started saving money. I realized that if I didn't get my act together, I'd probably find myself in trouble. I also got tired of owing people money and always having to ask people for stuff.
>
> I have a bank account and I put money in every chance I get. Let's say I get $20—$10 to $15 of that is going into my account.
>
> I know I may sound kind of preachy, but I'm telling the truth. Believe me, I've been there. Back in the day, I never saved money. I used to spend every little bit of money I got. All of it went to sneakers, video games, and comic books. The way I saw it, if you always saved your money, you'd never have anything.
>
> Having to repay the people who loaned me money is what made me see the light. I got tired of wasting my money. Why, summer before last I actually bought five pairs of sneakers—not because I needed them but just because I wanted to have every new pair that came out.

Nowadays, I try not to let styles affect me as much as they used to. I mean, they still do somewhat, but not to the extent of me not having any money in my pockets. Instead of buying five pairs of sneakers, I buy two or three and save the rest of my money. I manage my own bank account now and I work. Overall, I'd say I have my priorities in order.

I'm not telling you to put all your money in the bank for a rainy day. I'm also not going to lie and tell you that saving is easy, because it's not. It's the hardest thing to do in the world… well, in our age bracket anyway. But I can't go out of my house with empty pockets.

Although I know many of you won't take kindly to this, try to find ways to earn money. Go out into your neighborhood and walk dogs, mow lawns, shovel snow, pack bags. If none of my solutions appeal to any of you out there... improvise. For all it's worth, do whatever it takes to make some money.

And please don't take me literally on that. When I say, "Do whatever it takes," I don't mean to go out and rob and steal or sell drugs. Use your head, and make sure whatever you do is legal. Do the smart thing by looking out for your future.

Ralph didn't stop spending money or buying sneakers—he just cut down a bit and changed his money situation for the better.

Tip: Be Yourself

Patricia Rogers, 15, also found a way to develop good money habits—by being her own person:

High school is all about image. When teens come to school wearing $20 sneakers, they look like they don't care about what they have on or that they don't have enough money to afford the cooler brand names.

Clothing companies make us feel that we need their sneakers, jeans, and jackets to feel good about ourselves. When we don't buy those things, we sometimes feel bad about ourselves, especially when people look down on us and tease us.

And the pressure doesn't stop with the advertisers. As soon as teens see that other teens are wearing something with a name brand—no matter how ugly or expensive—we buy it.

I try to find nice clothes for a good price—by shopping for discounts. Every year my friends and I go shopping for inexpensive blue jeans and shirts in all colors. We don't go to the really expensive aisles, where jeans and shirts can cost $70 to $100. We go to the cheaper aisles and rack up on some plain jeans that cost $25 to $30. That way, we get more for our money and have enough clothes throughout the school year.

Tip: Separate Needs from Wants

Jeremiah Spears, 18, used to spend money like crazy until his friend Lisa made a great suggestion:

She suggested I make a chart of needs, wants and gotta-haves. Needs are like food, clothes (you don't want to walk down the street in your birthday suit), shoes, toothpaste (no one wants stinking breath, now do they?), etc.

Wants are things you can do without, but would rather not—like a car, a big house, more clothes, more shoes, jewelry.

Gotta-haves are really a way of spoiling yourself—they're things you see and decide you "must" have, like a pair of black snake-skin boots that I saw the other day. As you can imagine, gotta-haves tend to be more expensive.

Lisa said it's important to get what you need first and let the rest come later, so I began to make a chart every time I went shopping.

If you want to know where the slight edge is taking you, look at your habits and the kinds of choices you habitually make.

ACTION STEPS
- Which one of these suggestions could help you?
- How could you use it?

POINT #4: DON'T GIVE UP A HABIT—START A NEW ONE

It's tough to get rid of a habit you don't want—or to change anything—just through willpower. You can't just wish a habit away.

It's a lot easier to start a new habit. Eventually, the new habit becomes strong and replaces the old habit. That's what happened with Magda. She got over Mike by getting involved in new interests and activities. The new things she did became more interesting than feeling sorry for herself. And Magda did it the same way you do anything: one step at a time.

The first step in changing a habit is to know which one you want to change. One way to find out is to get into the habit of reflection.

Reflection means looking carefully at yourself and your life on a regular basis to see what you're happy with and what you want to change. You can reflect in many different ways—through writing or doing art, by taking long walks, by visiting a favorite place, talking to a favorite person, or through a religious or spiritual practice.

One teen, who wants to remain anonymous, used a journal to reflect on her feelings when her family was in a crisis.

When I was in the ninth grade, my mom lost her job and we didn't have any money to keep our apartment. My dad had left us and wasn't giving us financial support. I was really depressed (you can imagine how my mom felt) because I was concerned about my next meal and where I would sleep.

I wasn't really talking to anyone about what I was going through, which wasn't a good feeling. But because of all the stuff that was happening to me, I eventually started keeping a journal, which really helped me out. I gained a better understanding of how to handle emotional problems through writing in and re-reading my diary.

Writing allows my emotions to pour out of my emotional storage bag, my heart. When I hold my feelings in, I feel a lot

> It's tough to get rid of a habit you don't want. You can't just wish a habit away. It's a lot easier to start a new habit. Eventually, the new habit becomes strong and replaces the old habit.

of pressure and worry that I may eventually explode or take out my pain on someone else if the pressure is not released. But once my feelings are released, I feel at ease.

I began to write in my journal almost every day. After I poured out everything in those entries, I felt much better, even though I was still worried about what would happen to my mother.

Before I had my diary, I would just sit and cry and hope for the best when something bad happened. Sometimes I prayed, too. But writing helped me the most. My journal was my best friend. It made me think and helped me come up with different ways to handle problems by myself.

I now have over three years of my life recorded in my journal. I recently named it "Precious," because that's how I feel about all the thoughts it contains.

ACTION STEPS

- Do you take the time to reflect on your life?
- If so, how do you do it and what do you learn from it?
- If not, how could you begin to reflect on your life?

New, positive habits can bring you peace of mind. Writing, painting, drawing, walking, camping, exercising—all are ways to relax and calm yourself. Emily Orchier, 16, was very depressed until she started a new habit.

Have you ever been so depressed that you can't sleep, eat, or read? You have no friends to call and there's nothing good on TV. So you sigh, press your face into your pillow, and shed a few tears. This was my life two years ago. I had just turned 14 and I felt bleak.

One Saturday my mother peeked into my room on her regular "is Em still alive?" check. Even I knew that if I spent much more time like this, she would have to begin dusting me.

"Hi, hon," mom said.

I grunted in response.

"How are you feeling today, sweetheart?"

"How do you think?" I replied sarcastically.

Then my mother made her move:

"Emily! Get dressed! I'm taking the dog for a walk and you're coming with me!"

"Why?" I moaned.

"Because it will make you feel better."

The thought of moving was unbearable. I couldn't remember the last time I'd gone outside. Somehow I found the strength to slip on a pair of jeans and a black sweatshirt. My mother was waiting at the door for me, leash and dog in hand.

"I still don't get how going for a walk will make me feel any better," I complained.

My mother gave me a look and opened the door. We stepped outside. It was one of those unusually warm March days, but the signs of spring had yet to appear. It had been a long time since the warmth of the sun had touched my cheeks.

My mother led the dog and me to a dirt path that goes on for miles and miles. I carried on and complained the whole time we walked.

"This is boring, Mother. When can we go home?"

"Not just yet," she'd say.

My mother greeted every jogger, dog-walker, runner, and bicyclist who passed us by. She made herself happier than she really felt from being around me. I thought it was all so senseless. After walking for what seemed to be an eternity, she finally said that it was time to turn around.

When we got home, I felt as if a ton of bricks had been lifted from my heart. I didn't know how to handle it. For nearly a year I had been immersed in sadness. How could I learn to feel happy again? I soon found myself back in my room, in a comfortable funk.

Emily had fallen so deeply into the habit of being depressed that she didn't know how to be happy.

But that walk had done something to me. I didn't know how or why, but for a moment life almost felt all right. A week went by, and the next Saturday found me asking my mother if we could go for another walk.

April arrived and with it an array of beautiful spring blossoms. I began to take my dog out for her midmorning walks. We would go across the street to a big field, which led to small paths lined with daffodils, which in turn led to orchards with apple blossoms. Smaller fields abounded with blooming dogwood and magnolia trees, and scattered patches of tiny purple wildflowers. Walking there, I was overcome by beautiful fragrances. It became my little slice of heaven. I was healing.

So it came to pass that I was the official dog walker of the family. Walking became an everyday affair for me, and I began to acknowledge the powerful peace and relief that it brought me.

Late that summer, I remembered a small pond that my parents used to take me to when I was a very small child. One morning I decided to make the trek over there.

It was a very long walk, taking more than two hours there and back. But as soon as I laid eyes on the place, I knew that I loved it. Everywhere I looked there was life—ducks, geese, deer, turkeys, watersnakes, turtles, squirrels, and giant carp. I began to wake up early in the morning to take my daily pilgrimage there.

If walking was my spiritual practice, then that pond was my sanctuary. I felt such peace and serenity there. I also made many friends at the pond, and greeted every jogger, runner, dog-walker, or bicyclist who came my way.

Gradually, my depression lifted. Even though I've become much busier and have less time to walk, I make time to walk every day, if only for a little while. Walking saved me from my depression. It is strong medicine for the soul.

Sometimes, as Emily found out, it doesn't take a lot to turn your life around. Starting a new and positive habit—going to church on Sundays, volunteering for a worthy cause, calling an old friend, or just taking a walk—can lead to happiness.

ACTION STEPS

- Has this chapter given you an idea about starting a new habit?
- What is it?

Think About It

What Are Your Habits?

Think about the habits you have. Don't judge whether they're good or bad habits—that's not the point right now. Merely describe below the habits you have, in doing your schoolwork, relating to friends, deciding what to wear or eat, what music to listen to, or in any other area of your life.

_____

_____

_____

_____

_____

_____

_____

_____

Now, are there any habits you want to change? Again, don't judge them or put yourself down. Just list below the habits you'd like to try and change:

_____

_____

_____

_____

_____

_____

_____

Starting New Habits

Think about what you've read in this chapter. Reflect on changes you'd like to make in your life. But forget about changing old habits. Instead, what *new* habit or habits can you start in each area of your life?

New habits I can start for myself:

_____

_____

_____

_____

_____

New habits I can start with my friends:

_____

_____

_____

_____

_____

New habits I can start for my health (physical, mental, and spiritual):

_____

_____

_____

_____

_____

New habits I can start for my wealth:

_____

_____

_____

_____

_____

_____

New habits I can start for my education and career:

_____

_____

_____

_____

_____

New habits I can start for my impact on the world (my accomplishments or how I will be remembered):

_____

_____

_____

_____

_____

Which new habit would you like to start first? Can you start it today?

You're Always Learning

T he teens you've met in this book have faced a lot of challenges. And they've learned a lot from the challenges they've faced. That's what is so amazing and wonderful about this part of your life—you're always learning and discovering new things that have the power to put you on the path to success.

You may not think so, but you're in motion right now. You're either going up or going down. You're either flying, or falling. Because in life, you're never standing still.

Why is that?

Because the world is constantly changing and so are you. You're always in motion. Your life is always going somewhere. Everything changes. You aren't the same person today that you were yesterday. You won't be the same person tomorrow that you are today. You will have changed, even if only a tiny bit.

It can be pretty easy not to notice which direction you're going. It can look like you're standing still in one place, heading neither up nor down. But you're either on the path of continuous learning—or not on the path—whether you realize it or not.

Which way are you heading? You have total choice over that. But chances are, you don't realize it. The time when you have the most choice is now. The teen years are the best years for determining and changing the direction of your life. Once you get older, it can be a lot harder to find the time and freedom to go after the skills you want to acquire.

Perhaps this is a little scary. Perhaps you think you get one chance now and if you blow it, it's all downhill from here. Not at all. It only means that you have a great opportunity right now to set yourself on a course of continuous learning.

What does continuous learning mean? You probably have an idea, from what you've read so far.

It means there is no treading water in life, no running in place, no standing still. If you're not continually learning—if you're not taking advantage of opportunities to increase and use your knowledge—you're not on an upward path. And if you're not heading upward, you're heading in the other direction.

Continuous learning means:

▸ You haven't got it all figured out but are open to new possibilities. You're alert to finding opportunities in classes, programs, internships, and jobs.

▸ You try to develop your talents to the fullest by learning from people who have more experience than you do, usually adults. It means getting a team on your side, so you're not setting out on your journey alone.

▸ Most of all, it means continuously adjusting your course in life, as you learn from mistakes and apply what you've learned to new challenges and opportunities.

POINT #1: THE EARLIER YOU INVEST, THE GREATER THE REWARD

Your teen and young adult years are the time when you can begin molding yourself into the person you want to be, and let time work for you and be on your side. It's not that much different from the principle of compound interest, or how money grows over time.

The world of money is one of the easiest places to see the power of investing early. As we'll show you soon, the earlier you invest, the greater your reward.

One of your goals should be to put in place a financial plan for yourself so you are consistently, automatically building your savings. All this takes is choosing some simple action that is easy to do, which you repeat automatically, either daily, weekly, or monthly, and that will, over time, lead to financial success.

But financial success is not only about making money, but also about understanding how to make it and how to use it. That's what the following story is about.

You can be as wise and successful as the first boy. It's unlikely that anyone will ever give you a million dollars. But you can set up an automatic savings plan that

THE CHOICE

A wealthy man was about to die, so he called his twin sons to his bedside. The boys began to cry as they heard their father speak about his approaching death, but with a wave of his hand the father silenced them.

"I am leaving you both with a gift," he told his boys. "I want you to enjoy the same happiness I had during my long life. Which gift you choose is up to you."

The man reached into a beautiful box on his bedside table and held out two gifts. One gift was a thousand $1,000-dollar bills—a million dollars in cash. The other gift was a single, shiny copper penny.

"You both have the same choice—either one million or one penny. If you choose the million, it will be deposited in my bank in town and you can use it however you want. If you choose the penny, I will double the pennies you have every day for the next thirty-one days. Now, go rest and think. Come back tomorrow morning and tell me your choices."

He kissed them both and sent them on their way.

Late that night the first boy lay in bed thinking, "Why is our father giving us this choice? Which should I take?" He was unable to sleep. But the more he thought about his father's choices, the more he was sure about taking the penny.

The second son didn't lose any sleep. He had made his decision the moment his father had held out that sheaf of thousand-dollar bills. He was going to take the million dollars and he was already making big plans about what he was going to do with the money.

The next day the two boys went to see their father. The first son took the penny, and the second son took the million dollars.

A few days later, the boy decided to visit his brother, to see what he was doing with his penny.

"As father promised," the first son said, "my pennies have been doubling every day. On the second day, I had two pennies. On the third day, I had four pennies. On the fourth day, there were eight." The second son wasn't impressed. After all, he already had a million dollars and was sure to make a lot more.

Over the next weeks, the second son visited his brother every day and listened to him describe how his pennies were piling up. On Day 5, he had sixteen pennies; on Day 6, thirty-two; by week's end the boy had 64 cents. And by the end of the second week, he had $81.92.

A few days into the third week, the first son's pennies had grown to $655.35. But the second son was still not impressed.

On Day 28, the first boy's pennies had passed the million-dollar mark. On Day 29, he passed the two-and-a-half-million mark. On Day 30, his pennies totaled five million. And on Day 31, he had $10,737,418.24.

The boy who chose the penny had discovered the extraordinary power of *compound interest*—how money, even a very small amount of money—can grow over time.

The first son also understood that their father was giving them more than money.

The true gift was *wisdom* in knowing how to respect and use money.

The boy who chose the million had his $1 million. But the boy who chose the penny was worth more than *ten million dollars*. Because he wasn't greedy, because he was careful with his money, and because he understood how money can grow over time, he achieved true wealth.

The choice the wealthy man offered his two sons is the same choice the world offers you every day:

Small actions compound over time into big results.

The actions you take today, whether it's about money, friendships, or your health, can have a huge impact on your life over time.

will deduct, say, $10 a week from your paycheck or your checking account and deposit it into a savings account. That's $2 a day, not counting weekends.

Two dollars a day, $10 a week—that's about $500 a year. Let's say you're 16 years old and you start doing that now. What would happen in 30 years, by the time you reached the age of 46? Let's say you earned 5 percent interest a year on the money, which is a reasonable estimate.

Age	Payment	Total	Age	Payment	Total
16	$500	$ 525	32	500	$13,568
17	500	1,076	33	500	14,771
18	500	1,655	34	500	16,035
19	500	2,263	35	500	17,362
20	500	2,901	36	500	18,755
21	500	3,571	37	500	20,218
22	500	4,275	38	500	21,754
23	500	5,014	39	500	23,367
24	500	5,790	40	500	25,060
25	500	6,604	41	500	26,838
26	500	7,459	42	500	28,705
27	500	8,357	43	500	30,665
28	500	9,300	44	500	32,723
29	500	10,290	45	500	34,884
30	500	11,330	46	500	37,153
31	500	12,422			

More than $37,000—just by putting aside two bucks a day. Is that easy to do? Surprisingly so. Easy not to do? Tragically so. We've got a whole country full of people who aren't doing it and are ending up approaching retirement age wondering what they're going to live on.

The Cost of Putting It Off

"This saving thing seems like a great idea," you say, but for one reason or another (mainly because it's so easy *not* to do), you put it off. After all, not doing it doesn't hurt, right? It doesn't seem to have any real cost. You're only a teenager. You've got years ahead of you to start saving money.

But oh, what a cost. To give you a sense of the cost of waiting, look at the following example.

Remember Pauline Gordon back in Chapter Three? She just opened a retirement account at age 20 with $1,000. Let's say you have the same idea, and you and Pauline agree to each contribute $1,000 to your accounts each year (or $20 a week). This is for real—Pauline has already invested her first $1,000. But you don't get around to it. (Yes, it's an easy thing to do, but also pretty easy *not* to do.) You don't start this year, or next year, or the next. In fact, you keep putting it off for the next six years.

But at the beginning of Year Seven, when you ask Pauline how she's doing, you can't believe her reply: *she's already finished!*

After investing $1,000 a year for six years at 12%, she's all set. All she has to do is let it sit there and accumulate interest, without adding any new savings. By the time she reaches age sixty, the little financial ball she's started rolling will have snowballed into over $500,000—even if she never puts in another dime.

So you decide to catch up and start putting away $20 a week, or $1,000 a year. At what age will your savings top $500,000, so you can stop putting in that weekly $20 like Pauline did?

Let's do the math...

A Delay of Six Little Years

Age	Pauline		You	
	Payment	Total	Payment	Total
19	$ 1,000	$ 1,120	0	0
20	1,000	2,374	0	0
21	1,000	3,779	0	0
22	1,000	5,353	0	0
23	1,000	7,115	0	0
24	1,000	9,089	0	0
25	0 *(Pauline stops)*	10,180	$ 1,000	$ 1,120
26	0	11,401	1,000	2,374
27	0	12,769	1,000	3,779
28	0	14,302	1,000	5,353

Age	Pauline		You	
	Payment	Total	Payment	Total
29	0	16,018	1,000	7,115
30	0	17,940	1,000	9,089
31	0	20,093	1,000	11,300
32	0	22,504	1,000	13,776
33	0	25,205	1,000	16,549
34	0	28,229	1,000	19,655
35	0	31,617	1,000	23,133
36	0	35,411	1,000	27,029
37	0	39,660	1,000	31,393
38	0	44,419	1,000	36,280
39	0	49,749	1,000	41,753
40	0	55,719	1,000	47,884
41	0	62,406	1,000	54,750
42	0	69,894	1,000	62,440
43	0	78,281	1,000	71,052
44	0	87,675	1,000	80,699
45	0	98,196	1,000	91,503
46	0	109,980	1,000	103,603
47	0	123,177	1,000	117,155
48	0	137,959	1,000	132,334
49	0	154,514	1,000	149,334
50	0	173,055	1,000	168,374
51	0	193,822	1,000	189,699
52	0	217,081	1,000	213,583
53	0	243,130	1,000	240,333
54	0	272,306	1,000	270,293
55	0	304,983	1,000	303,848
56	0	341,581	1,000	341,429
57	0	382,570	1,000	383,521
58	0	428,479	1,000	430,663
59	0	479,896	1,000	483,463
60	0	537,484	1,000	542,599

You can't believe your eyes—you're not going to catch up to Pauline until you turn 57! That six years of procrastination has cost you *36 years* of investing. That's 30 *more* years than it would have taken, and $30,000 more that you would have had to invest, just to wind up at the same place. If only you had started when Pauline did!

And by the way—in case your dad is reading this, or someone else in their 50s or 60s, and they're slapping their foreheads and moaning that they wished they'd done this in their teens, tell them to relax: It's not too late. You're *never* too old and it's *never* too late to start applying the slight edge to achieve your dreams.

The point here is that there is a cost to waiting—whether it's money or developing the attitude and skills you need to succeed. It's never too late to start. But it's *always* too late to wait. And the earlier you start, the better.

While this is true about money (and knowing how to handle your money is a very good thing), early investing is not much different with all the other areas of your life. Right now, in your teen years, you have the power and the freedom to invest in where your life will head in the long run. Right now is the best time for setting your life on the right course. Habits, actions, attitudes, and philosophy—you know by now how powerful they are. The earlier you can get on the right track in all of these areas, the better. Putting it off is not the way to go.

What you're going to do with your life is much more than a question of what kind of job you'll have or how much money you'll make (although both are important). It's a question of deciding what kind of person you want to be. Now is the time to decide and take action.

ACTION STEPS
- Do you have a plan for saving money?
- In what other ways could you invest in your future?

POINT #2: TAKE ADVANTAGE OF ALL OPPORTUNITIES

Continuous learning means taking advantage of all opportunities, as Tonya Groover did when she was a teen:

As soon as I was able to work, I always had a job. I just didn't sit around the house after school. I took the bus to the mall and worked at the mall.

You develop those habits and discipline through after school jobs and extracurricular activities.

If you see an opportunity, grab it. That was my thing. Whenever I saw something free—free was my favorite word. If I saw a free program, I was involved in it.

Desiree took advantage of a journalism internship in high school that exposed her to the working world:

It helped to broaden my horizons. I was interviewing people and seeing how the professional world works. It taught me to think differently about myself. When you see examples of success, it makes it tangible and gives you something to reach for. It helps you to be comfortable in a working atmosphere. And it helps you to know how to get things that you want.

Andrea Facey, 18, had an opportunity to learn about the business world and grabbed it:

Last summer I was accepted into the summer program of the National Foundation for Teaching Entrepreneurship (NFTE). The goal of NFTE is to teach people the basics of how to start a business.

At our first meeting, we were given information about the business world. Then we were asked to write up descriptions for the businesses we wanted to start. I planned to sell goods related to Caribbean culture (I'm from Jamaica) and call my business Caribbean Heat.

To write the description, I had to think like a consumer. I had to decide what I liked to buy and what other young people would be interested in buying. I had to come up with prices that would be competitive with stores that sell Caribbean items. I also had to estimate what my profits would be over a one-year period.

Later on in the week, we were each given $25 to buy things that we wanted to sell. My friends Takiesha and Michelle bought cosmetics and earrings. I bought things that represented my Caribbean culture, like rasta belts, pouches, and chains. I also bought crystal chains, lighters, spandex, and cologne.

After that shopping spree, we went back to the office to demonstrate our sales pitches—what you say to customers to persuade them to buy your products. We had to get in front of video cameras and do our sales pitches. I was nervous at first and it got worse when I couldn't get one of the lighters to work. Then we watched the tape to see what we could do better.

I learned that I had to speak more slowly. I seemed to rush through my lines. And the incident with the lighter taught me that I have to check my merchandise before showing it to customers.

Next, we discussed different ways to design our business cards. We had to think of creative slogans to catch the attention of customers. I thought of this for my card:

CARIBBEAN HEAT "Come fi de nuf nice stuff"
Andrea Facey
President
Rasta belts, pouches, lighters, etc.

To encourage us to save our money, we were given the opportunity to open bank accounts with a $25 contribution from NFTE. We received receipt books to keep track of how much money we made.

After the program ended, I decided to try to keep running my business. It's going slow but I'm making a little money for myself. So far the items that are really selling are the rasta belts, pouches, and the map pendants of Africa.

The hardest part of being an entrepreneur is the competition of the different businesses around you. Some customers try to get you to lower your prices because someone else is selling that same item for less. You have to make sure the customer doesn't feel like she's being ripped off.

And, of course, finances are always a problem. You have to have money to start a business and keep it going, especially if you are selling things that need to be restocked.

Despite the problems, I'm glad I had this opportunity to get a peek into the real world. The experience of starting my own business opened my eyes to possible careers later on in my life.

ACTION STEPS

- What opportunities do you have available to you right now?
- What new opportunities would you like to have?
- How could you go about getting them?

POINT #3: YOU NEED A TEAM ON YOUR SIDE

In order to continuously learn, you need help. We've got this "do-it-yourself, I-don't-need-anyone" idea in America, like it's somehow cooler, tougher, smarter, or better to do things on your own (and only for yourself).

But doing it all by yourself is not only unnecessary but impossible. You *can't* do it on your own. So how do you get the help you need?

Everyone needs someone they can confide in, someone they can talk to about whatever mountains they happen to be facing at the time. "Someone you can talk to" might mean a professional counselor, but not necessarily. It might be an uncle, a grandparent, a teacher, a school counselor, or a coach.

When Giselle John found an adult to confide in, her life changed. She came to the U.S. from Trinidad and Tobago at age 14 and had a rough time adjusting to high school. She got into a fight with another girl just two weeks after she started ninth grade, and soon lost all interest in her education.

> *I kept getting low grades because I was cutting and not doing the work. Sometimes I would just go home and sleep, or I wouldn't even go to school at all. There was no one looking over me, so I did what I wanted. I failed almost all my exams.*
>
> *I didn't live with my family because they were back in the West Indies. I lived with my mom's friend, and she was too busy with her own life to pay attention to mine.*
>
> *Then I found a babysitting job, which made things worse. I was always tired and skipping school more often than before. I couldn't give up the job. I needed the money to take care of myself.*

But when Giselle began the 10th grade, she met a teacher who would change her life.

> *One day I was falling asleep in my English classroom. Just before the period ended I woke up, only to see my teacher, Ms. Stanford, looking at me.*
> *"What's the matter with you?" she asked.*
> *"Nothing," I answered softly.*
> *I wanted to tell her what was on my mind. I needed someone to listen to me and I knew she would. I always noticed how the other kids related to her. She*

was friendly but stern. The other kids seemed to like her, even those students she failed numerous times. I thought I could relate to her.

At the end of the class, I approached her table and asked if I could speak to her whenever she had time. She said yes and we made plans to see each other at lunch that same day.

That meeting was a turning point for Giselle.

I told her what was bothering me and she listened. After that day I went to see her at lunch almost every day. We began to walk home because we lived in the same direction.

I could talk to her about anything that bothered me, and she always gave me good advice. She understood me because she was from the West Indies, too. (Ms. Stanford is from Guyana.) She took an interest in my life and I felt special. She even took me to church. I began to settle down and go to school more often.

Ms. Stanford once told me that even before she knew me personally, she tried to get me out of regular English and into honors English, because she knew regular English was no challenge for me. I felt good when she told me that because I never saw myself as a good student.

It meant that I had potential and I was smart. I felt intelligent and wanted to prove that I could do well in school. I wanted to get good grades and be on the honor roll. I wanted to be somebody in life—the lawyer I dreamt of being ever since I was younger. I was hardly ever late or absent from school. Eventually, I got placed in more honors classes.

I made new friends as I changed classes, and they were kids who were hard workers. Many of my old friends either left school, changed school, got expelled, or just hung out in the hallways. My new friends were looking toward the future and so was I. Instead of hanging out and cutting school, we were studying to pass an exam and to stay on the honor roll.

My friendship with Mrs. Stanford has lasted throughout the years. Presently we still attend the same church, a place I forgot when I came to this country.

Eventually Giselle graduated near the very top of her high school class, which wouldn't have been possible without Mrs. Stanford's help.

Another way to get support is to find a mentor.

There are three ways to learn something new.

- One is to study how it works and what to do.
- The second is to learn by actually doing it.
- But, there is a third and even more powerful way to learn, and that is to find someone else who's already mastered something you want to do. That person, called a mentor, can teach you through his or her experience.

Pauline Gordon has made use of mentors for several years:

> I have two mentors who help me. Both are business majors and they helped me with my résumé. If I have to do a cover letter, I do a rough draft and let them edit it. And sometimes they look over my résumé. Every time I apply for a job I always feel confident because I have that network and that support. And my résumé is great.
>
> There are so many resources out there that you just need to take advantage of. And networking is very important—for example, talking to your teachers after school or going to the guidance counselor.

Whatever goals you aspire to, seek out adults who have achieved the same or very similar goals. Hang out with people who have been there and done that. If you want to be a good writer, spend time with good writers. If you want to be a success in business, then find a way to spend time with a successful business-person. If you want to be a painter, study with an adult artist. If you're thinking of becoming a lawyer, set up a meeting to talk with an attorney. There are many adults out there who have a lot of skills and knowledge to share.

ACTION STEPS

- What kind of support do you need in your life right now?
- Is there an adult who could give you that support?
- How can you find that person?

POINT #4: ADJUST YOUR COURSE CONTINUALLY

When you drive a car, you're constantly making tiny adjustments, correcting the direction you're heading every moment. Once you've learned to drive, that constant adjustment of the steering wheel becomes so familiar that it's second nature, and you probably never think about it. But if you decided to hold the wheel in one place, you'd be off the road in less than a minute.

Perhaps you think being off course is something to avoid at all costs. After all, if you're off course, you're failing, right? Not according to the slight edge. Remember Thomas Watson Sr.'s philosophy:

> *Would you like me to give you the formula for success? It's quite simple, really.* Double your rate of failure. *You're thinking of failure as the enemy of success. But it isn't at all. So go ahead and make mistakes. Make all you can. Because that's where you'll find success: on the other side of failure.*

The Apollo spacecraft didn't reach the moon safely because it was always on target—it achieved its destination by constantly correcting its course. Planes do the same thing. So do babies, when they're learning how to walk. And so do successful teens.

Desiree had to adjust course when she arrived at college, as almost all students have to do. She felt out of place among students who had gone to private schools, because she had always gone to public schools:

> *I had this whole image of what college was like in my head. I was really excited, but at the same time a little bit nervous, a little bit scared. There were lots of kids with a private school education and I'm from a public school.*
>
> *It's all about realizing they're not too different from you. Of course there are going to be people who were exposed to more things than you were, but there are other people who weren't. Sometimes you'll be more knowledgeable about an aspect of life than someone else. At the beginning people were showing off because we all had the same fear. Now we're comfortable around each other because we've all found where we belong. And we all realize that we each have something special to offer.*

Samantha Brown, 17, had to adjust course when she opened her first bank account. She wanted her own account, but had to open a joint account with her mother, which meant that both Samantha and her mother could put in and take out money, whenever they wanted, without consulting each other. Samantha felt like her mother didn't trust her.

I sucked in my breath so I wouldn't start to cry. I felt like my one chance at independence was taken right out of my hands. It didn't seem like my bank account, it seemed like my mother's.

The bank teller and my mother both stared at me, waiting for my reaction. I just smiled dryly and said, "OK, no problem." But in the pit of my stomach I was nauseated that I needed my mother's signature to have this account.

For a while I liked the freedom of having an account, with money that was there any time I needed it—especially since my mom was really cheap when it came to giving me allowance. Actually, I was cheap, too, when it came to spending it. I hated spending my money—even on myself. I was afraid that if I let myself start spending it, I'd wind up spending the whole thing. So I was very responsible with my money. If I took money out of the bank to buy something, I would immediately save up some more and put it back.

Everything was going well, until Samantha was in her sophomore year of high school.

I was going away for a big track meet, and I needed $100 for admissions, plus money for food and clothing to wear. When the track meet came around, I wanted to show my mother that I could go without begging her for money. So I took about $200 out of my account. I told myself that I would eventually get a job and put the money back in.

But when my mother found out that I was going to the meet, she gave me money too. Instead of putting it in the bank to replace the money I took out, I used it to buy more clothing—for school, for the summer, and even just to have more clothes. I bought a lot of jeans, one for every day of the week. I bought five of the same shirts, each a different color. I bought cardigans with corduroy skirts to match, and little tees and dresses. I even went as far as to buy church dresses—though I hardly ever go to church.

I just went wild.

But when September came, along came the big expenses. First it was the PSAT, then the SAT, then the SAT again. I needed money fast, so I went back into my account for more money. When I saw I had only about $200 left, I panicked. I thought, "If my mother finds out, she'll take my bank book away."

I began searching my room for money that I had stored up. I saved my allowance. I even tracked down friends who owed me a dollar or fifty cents.

I was able to pay off my expenses and replace the money I had wasted—which was a relief.

Even though I had to sweat and panic to put the money back, I still think the experience was worth it. I was able to see a bit what the real world would be like and what I would be up against. I got to learn about myself and see how I reacted. I learned that I'm not always the super-responsible person I thought I was.

But it also made me see that I was able to get out of a bad situation on my own.

I believe if adults trusted teens a little more and gave us a chance to screw up and learn from our mistakes, we'd probably be more cautious when spending our money.

ACTION STEPS

- Are there ways that you need to "adjust course" in your life? Are there ways you need to change the way you see things or do things?

- What are they? What steps could you take to adjust your course?

Think About It

Take Advantage of Opportunities

What new skills or new opportunities would you like to have? Jot down your thoughts below.

_____

_____

_____

_____

_____

_____

_____

Find a Mentor

A mentor is an adult who can help you learn a skill or gain a certain kind of knowledge.

Is there an adult who can help you achieve what you want? Who is that person? What would you like to learn from him or her?

_____

_____

_____

_____

_____

_____

Adjust Your Course

Are there ways you need to "adjust course" in your life? To change the way you see things or do things? What are they?

_____

_____

_____

_____

_____

_____

_____

What steps could you take to adjust your course?

_____

_____

_____

_____

_____

_____

_____

Make Your Dreams
Come True

You've got seven ways to apply the slight edge to everything you do:

▶ The little things you do matter.
▶ Your attitude is everything.
▶ The present moment is all you have.
▶ It takes small steps to get where you're going.
▶ Failure is your best friend.
▶ Good habits are your next best friend.
▶ You're always learning.

Now it's time to go deeper and make your dreams come true. At the beginning of this book, we asked you to imagine your dream life. In this last chapter, it's time to look at how to turn those dreams into reality.

It's time to plan your future and think about your dreams. To reflect on the things you have experienced and how they have affected you.

▶ What have you learned from your past experiences? How have you grown?
▶ How do you need to continue to grow?
▶ What areas in your life do you need to work on?
▶ What are your goals and how are you going to achieve them?
▶ What have you learned from the stories in this book that can help you?

By now you know that success is no accident. Teens who achieve what they want in life do it by following a very specific recipe. Perhaps they're not even aware that they've taken specific steps, but everyone who has ever created success in their lives, whether consciously or not, has followed more or less the same process.

And to reach the specific and tangible goals that make up success, there are four steps you need to follow. For any goal to come true:

- You must picture it vividly.
- You must look at it every day.
- You must have a plan to start with.
- You can't quit on yourself.

Let's go through those steps one by one.

STEP ONE: PICTURE IT VIVIDLY

The most important skill for creating success in anything is the skill of *envisioning.* Envisioning means creating a picture of something that hasn't actually happened yet, but making that picture so vivid that it feels real.

The reason this is so crucial is that your subconscious mind—remember, that part of you that controls 99.99 percent of what unfolds in your life— needs a clear picture of your destination. Once you have a clear, vivid picture imprinted in your mind, you'll find a route to get there.

It doesn't work the other way around—you don't pick out roads that look good and hope they'll take you to the right place. Destination has to come first. To create your dream life, you have to start with some sort of vivid picture of where it is you're headed. You start with the end in mind.

Pick a dream you have, any dream—an accomplishment, a triumph, your dream house, dream car, dream job, the relationship of your dreams. Pick a dream that you'd *really* like to have come true. Look back at the answers that you wrote after each chapter. Keep picking until you have five dreams. Write them out in the space on page 120.

As you do, here are some tips to follow.

- Write your dreams in the present tense and don't use any words that make your dreams seem vague or not realistic. For example, don't write "I hope to" or "I'll try to" or "If possible." Instead, write "I will…"

This is important because your subconscious doesn't deal with the future—it deals in the *now*. If you write out, "Someday I hope to be an elementary school teacher" or "Someday I hope to write a novel," that goal won't be real in your subconscious. It's better to write something like, "I will be proud to be an elementary school teacher" or "I will be successful in writing a novel." It even helps to say your goals out loud.

This might seem a little awkward or goofy to you. Saying out loud, "I have discovered a cure for cancer" may feel funny, when the current truth is that you have no idea what causes cancer. That's okay. If it feels funny, let it feel funny. This is where dreams start.

▸ Make your dream vivid. Envisioning isn't simply creating a picture in your mind. That's wishful thinking. Envisioning means *making it real.* You need to make it *physical,* and that involves your senses. The more vivid it is, the more it starts to become real.

CREATE A DREAM BOARD

One way to make your dream vivid is to find a bunch of pictures that represent the things you want to accomplish and make them into a collage. You can cut pictures out of magazines, print them off the Internet, or take photos of things you want. You can then thumbtack them to a corkboard or glue them to cardboard. This is called a "dream board" and it's a great way to make your dreams seem real and reachable.

For example, if your dream is to own a home, describe it in vivid detail. How many rooms does it have? What does the yard look like? What kind of living room or kitchen? What's the neighborhood like?

▸ Don't worry about doing this "right." There are no right answers. You're flexing your dream muscles. Your dreams can be anything—as huge as stopping global warming or as modest as getting an A in math next year. The size of the dream doesn't matter. The only requirement is that these dreams are *real* for you.

Now start:

My Five Dreams

1. _____

_____

_____

2. _____

_____

_____

3. _____

_____

_____

4. _____

_____

_____

5. _____

_____

_____

Make Your Dreams as Specific as Possible

Now, do two things that will make your dreams even more concrete. Look at each dream you wrote down and ask two questions.

The first question is, "What, exactly?" Go back to each dream, one at a time, and add whatever wording you need to make sure each goal is *specific*.

Why is that important?

Let's say you wrote down, "Good grades next year." But what exactly is a good grade for you? Does that mean straight A's? Does that mean going from a C average to a B average? Does it mean good grades in specific subjects?

If you wrote down, "Get a job and make money," what does that actually mean? What kind of job? How much money? What will you do with that money? Spend it? Put it in a bank account?

What if you wrote down "Be more healthy"? Does that mean eating better? If so, eating what exactly? Getting more exercise? Stopping smoking?

Imagine reading your dreams out loud to someone you care about, and that person saying, "I'm not quite sure what you mean. Can you tell me exactly what you're shooting for?"

Rewrite the same five dreams below, only this time add whatever words you need to make each one as specific as possible. Picture it vividly—and make that picture *real* and *here* and *now*.

My Five Dreams in More Detail

1. _____

_____

_____

_____

_____

_____

_____

_____

2. _____

_____

_____

_____

_____

_____

3. _____

_____

_____

_____

_____

_____

4. _____

_____

_____

_____

_____

5. _____

_____

_____

_____

_____

_____

When Will You Accomplish Your Dreams?

The next question is, "By when?" It's easy to put things off until later. But if you set a specific time to accomplish your dreams, you'll be less likely to put them off.

Goals are dreams with deadlines. Let's reshape your dreams into goals by putting a date on each one. In the spaces below, write out each of those five dreams one more time, this time adding words that answer the question, "By when?"

I Will Accomplish My Five Dreams By...

1. _____

_____

_____

_____

2. _____

_____

_____

_____

3. _____

_____

_____

4. _____

_____

_____

_____

5. _____

_____

_____

_____

STEP TWO: LOOK AT IT EVERY DAY

If life were a sprint, you could run it with your conscious mind. But life is not a sprint—it's a marathon. It's not a matter of the first step you take, or even the second, or even the third. There are thousands of steps that follow when you work toward your goals, and each one gives you the opportunity to get off course and lose your way.

Whether you stay on the path you want or get distracted and veer off is a question of how you've programmed your subconscious mind. And one of the best ways to program yourself to stay on the path is through repetition—by showing your subconscious your dreams every day. It's the same reason you want to keep yourself in the company of positive people: You need to avoid the temptations that can lead you astray.

As a young child, you probably heard a lot more no's than yesses. Picturing your dream or looking at your dream board every day is like feeding your subconscious with a diet rich in yesses.

It's not enough to just make a picture: Once you've got your picture, wrap it around yourself and immerse yourself in it.

So how do you do that? In addition to rereading your dreams or creating a dream board, you can also make a declaration. A declaration is simply a positive statement about achieving your dream. For example, "I will finish college by the time I'm 21 and begin my career as a teacher." Or, "I am going to apply myself to writing and will finish a collection of poetry by my 18th birthday."

In the space below, write out a list of declarations that you can say to yourself every day about each of your five dreams.

My Dream Declarations

1. _____

_____

_____

2. _____

_____

_____

3. _____

_____

_____

4. _____

_____

_____

5. _____

_____

_____

STEP THREE: START WITH A PLAN

Making a plan is where people are often thrown off track. You may be worried that if you don't make the right plan, the plan won't work. And that can seem scary. How will you know whether it'll work or not?

You don't know. Nobody does. But knowing whether it'll work or not doesn't matter. The point is not to come up with a plan that you know is a sure thing. The point is simply to come up with a plan that will get you started.

Let's hear from Xavier Reyes about making plans:

> How many times have you heard an adult ask you what your goals are? And how many times did you answer that you didn't know, or just gave them any old answer that would shut them up?
>
> As annoying as this question may seem, it's a very important one. If we didn't have goals, we would be like drivers without destinations, driving round and round without really going anywhere. Goals help us focus on our dreams and realize the possibilities in our lives. Goals let us be in the driver's seat for a change.
>
> When I was 17, one of my goals was to live on my own. In order to achieve my goals, I had to make sure that I had two very important things: a roof over my head, and a secure job that was going to pay enough for rent.
>
> It took years of work to reach those goals. I had to learn how to find and hold down a job. I had to look for apartments and convince landlords that I would

be a responsible tenant. I was eventually able to get a job as an administrative director in an office. I found an apartment through my social worker's assistant.

If I hadn't had goals and a game plan for how I was going to reach them, I wouldn't be where I am today. I wouldn't have my own apartment and I sure wouldn't have my job. I might have made it, but I probably would have been working for half of the salary I now make, and would be living in a studio apartment the size of a closet.

So here's another important thing about reaching your goals—it's not just enough to have a goal, you also have to have a game plan, which is a plan for how and when you're going to reach those goals. For instance, to find an apartment, my game plan was to look in the classified sections of newspapers, ask everyone I knew about apartments, and get together all the things a landlord would want to see—references, paycheck stubs, savings account statements and a Social Security card.

But having goals and a game plan is just half of it. The other half is actually putting the game plan into action. And if you're like me, this is the hard part— getting off our butts and doing what we need to do to reach our goals. Before you begin to work on a game plan for reaching your dreams, it's important to know the difference between a strong goal and a weak goal, a realistic goal and an unrealistic goal.

Weak goals are goals that you are going to achieve whether or not you really put work into it.

The more specific you are in your goal, the clearer it will be, and the more likely it is that you will get exactly what you want (and not half of it).

An unrealistic goal is to say that you want to be a doctor by the time you are 23, knowing that you are 17 and haven't even begun studying medicine. A realistic goal is to say that you want to be in medical school (or whatever school you want) by the time you are 23. This is realistic because you are giving yourself enough time to get the education and experience you need to reach your goal.

A good, strong goal is one that is measurable, that is very clear, and that is achievable. The more specific and focused your goal, the better the chance you will have of reaching it.

But once you have your goals, you need a game plan.

It's up to you to take the necessary steps to achieve your goals. No one is going to give you a break or a free handout. If you want something, get up and make it happen for yourself. You can do it.

You have to start somewhere. You have to start with a plan. But the plan you start with will not be the plan that gets you there. Your plan will have to change over and over again. You'll meet obstacles. The unexpected will happen. You'll have to adjust course, because you'll be continuously learning.

You might be wondering, "Then why bother? If my plan isn't going to get me there, why make one in the first place?"

Because the plan gives you a place to begin. You need a plan in the same way you need a dollar to start a bank account. The way you took your first baby step. The way you struggled to sound out the first sentence you ever read. Without that dollar, that first wobbling step, or that first stumbling sentence, your dream—no matter how deeply you want it—will never become reality.

Don't make the mistake of thinking you need a perfect plan. There is no perfect plan. There can't be, because a plan is not the same as getting there—it's only your starting point. If you put too much energy into trying to make your plan perfect, you're more likely to take all the life and joy out of doing it.

Don't try to figure it all out. Whatever you can dream, you can do. So do it! Write out your plan for each dream below, being as specific as you can.

My Plan for Reaching My Dreams

1. _____

_____

_____

_____

_____

_____

_____

2. _____

_____

_____

_____

_____

_____

3. _____

_____

_____

_____

_____

_____

4. _____

_____

_____

_____

_____

5. _____

_____

_____

_____

_____

STEP FOUR: DON'T QUIT ON YOURSELF

What is the real point of the story about the tortoise and the hare? "Slow and steady wins the race," right? But in reality, going slow is not always better. Sometimes you can move too slowly. Sometimes fast is better. If you're crossing a street and a car is coming fast, forget the tortoise. Sometimes fast is the right strategy. Sometimes slow is. Sometimes it changes. The key word is not *slow* but *steady*.

Steady wins the race. That's the truth of it.

Jacob Suarez, 16, puts it this way:

> *I used to try to just get by doing the bare minimum. It took a while to get in the mindset of going the extra mile. Like every time I used to get on the computer, it was tempting to go on the Internet and spend an hour looking at random stuff. It takes a lot of good discipline and habits and boundaries to use that time in other ways.*
>
> *But once you go the extra mile, things become easier to do. You can get on a roll and keep going. And it's not that much more effort to go the second mile than if you were doing the bare minimum, because habit has a momentum to it.*

Jacob used the key word: *momentum*. The fable of the tortoise and the hare is really about the remarkable power of momentum.

We know from physics that a body at rest tends to stay at rest—and a body in motion tends to remain in motion. That's why the small things you do every day are so important. Once you're in motion, it's easy to keep in motion. Once you stop, it's hard to get going again.

Let's say you and your friend both want to learn to play an instrument over the summer, well enough so you can play together in the fall. It doesn't matter what instrument—guitar, drums, violin, banjo, you name it. You agree to practice a half-hour every day. But your friend gets busy with other things and figures, "Hey, half an hour times seven is three and a half hours, right? Instead of doing my half-hour every day, I'm going to practice four hours every Sunday." At the end of the summer, who's going to know how to play the instrument?

It won't be your friend.

Why not? Week after week, the same thing happens to your friend all summer: after six days off, every Sunday feels like he's starting all over again. By not practicing for six days, he's lost whatever ground he gained—he's lost all his momentum.

But if you work every day toward your goals, it takes less energy to get started every day. And once you've gotten started and you're in a rhythm, it takes a whole lot less energy to *keep* yourself going.

There's another reason a little every day is far better than a lot once a week. The daily rhythm of habits starts to change you. As it becomes part of your routine, it becomes part of who you are. That doesn't happen with a once-in-a-while, all-out effort.

To give you another example, imagine taking a 20-minute brisk walk in the morning before school, and then after school working out for another 20 minutes. Imagine you did that every day for a week. How would you feel at the end of the week?

But what if you decided to do the whole week's worth of exercise on just one day each week. What if you took a 140-minute walk (that's over two hours!) in the morning and in the afternoon spent another 140 minutes working out—and then did nothing for the next six days. How well would that work?

Steady wins the race.

Think about your five dreams. Now, for each dream, think of small steps you can take each day to begin making them come true.

Small Steps I Can Take Every Day to Reach My Dreams

1. _____

_____

_____

_____

_____

_____

2. _____

_____

_____

_____

_____

_____

3. _____

_____

_____

_____

_____

_____

4. _____

_____

_____

_____

_____

_____

5. _____

_____

_____

_____

_____

_____

Start pursuing your dreams today!

Afterword

If God had meant man to fly, he would have given him wings.
—*Bishop Milton Wright*

Why can't people fly? Because life can seem pretty heavy. That's just the way it is. That's the way Bishop Milton Wright saw it.

The founder of Huntingdon College in Indiana, Bishop Wright delivered a sermon in 1090, pointing out a truth that everyone at the time knew:

"If God had meant man to fly, he would have given him wings."

But some people don't accept the same "truths" other people accept. Some people just don't buy the idea that our lives are held down by gravity. Some people get the crazy idea into their heads that they're going to go as far as the success curve will take them, even if it means doing things that no one else can imagine.

For example, take Bishop Wright's two sons.

Thirteen years after Wright preached that sermon, Wilbur and Orville Wright built and flew the first successful airplane. The Wright brothers somehow knew a truth that most people never realize: God *did* mean us to fly. That's why he gave us wings. And we've been getting ready to use them since the day we were born. But as we grow up, most of us have forgotten we have them.

The slight edge is your key *to regaining your* wings—to realize you've always had them and can use them to soar as high as you want.

Picture the dream life you want to live, find the best ways to take the first step, and then the second, and then the third, and learn to stay on course. Before long—perhaps a lot sooner than you expect—you'll be in full flight.

The Slight Edge Principles

The slight edge philosophy comes down to this: You can create any life you want, no matter how difficult it may seem, but only by understanding how small, positive steps make a difference over time. The things you do every single day—things that don't look like such a big deal or like they don't even matter—*do* matter.

Here are the main points of the slight edge:

- **Little Things Matter:** The little things you do every day, whether positive or negative, will determine what kind of life you lead.

- **Attitude Is Everything:** Your actions are driven by what you most deeply believe about yourself and the world.

- **Use the Moment:** You can create a better future by spending less time in the past and taking action in the present.

- **Everything Starts with Small Steps:** Every success in life, large or small, starts and continues with small steps.

- **There's No Such Thing As Failure:** Success is built on failure, because it helps you discover your strengths and creates unexpected opportunities.

- **Habits Are Powerful:** Positive habits are powerful tools that can help you reach your full potential.

- **You're Always Learning:** There's no standing still in life, as you always have opportunities to learn something new.

- **You Can Make Your Dreams into Reality:** By taking small, positive steps over time, your dreams can come true.

Resources for Teens

BOOKS AND AUDIOS

As a Man Thinketh, James Allen

A Fortune to Share, Paul J. Meyer

Life Strategies for Teens, Jay McGraw

The Magic of Thinking Big, Dr. David J. Schwartz

The Power of Positive Thinking, Norman Vincent Peale

The Seasons of Life, Jim Rohn

The 7 Habits of Highly Effective People, Stephen Covey

The 7 Habits of Highly Effective Teens, Sean Covey

The Six Most Important Decisions You'll Ever Make, Sean Covey

The Slight Edge: Secret to a Successful Life, Jeff Olson

Success Through a Positive Mental Attitude, W. Clement Stone

Teens Can Make It Happen, Stedman Graham

Think and Grow Rich, Napoleon Hill

You Call the Shots, Cameron Johnson and John David Mann

You Can If You Think You Can, Norman Vincent Peale

ORGANIZATIONS

Activism 2000 Project
National organization that encourages youth to become involved in community issues related to health, education, the environment, crime, and other problems. **www.youthactivism.com**

Americorps
Offers volunteer opportunities in nearly 1,000 national or local programs that address community needs in education, public safety, human services, and the environment. **www.americorps.org**

Boys & Girls Clubs of America
Provides programs in leadership development, education and career exploration, financial literacy, health and life skills, the arts, sports, fitness and recreation, and family outreach. **www.bgca.org**

Boy Scouts of America
One of the nation's largest character-development and leadership training programs for youth, serving more than 4.6 million young people between 7 and 20 years of age. **www.scouting.org**

The College Board
An all-in-one Web site that offers information on colleges, scholarships, the SATs and PSATs, and careers. **www.collegeboard.com**

Do Something
A national nonprofit organization that involves young people in activism and community leadership. **www.dosomething.org**

Earth Force
Helps young people discover and implement solutions to environmental problems in their communities. The organization is youth-driven, with a national Youth Advisory Board made up of members ages 10-17. **www.earthforce.org**

EPA Student Center
Offers students in middle and high school the chance to explore a wide range of environmental issues, including information on awards, scholarships, internships, club projects, and fun activities. **www.epa.gov/students**

Girl Scouts of America
Girl Scouts is the world's preeminent organization dedicated solely to girls where character-building and success skills are taught, such as leadership, strong values, social conscience, and conviction about their own potential and self-worth. **www.girlscouts.org**

Habitat for Humanity
Brings volunteers and communities together to build affordable housing. It offers a weeklong service program for high school and college students. **www.habitat.org**

Junior Achievement
World's largest organization dedicated to inspiring and preparing young people to succeed in the global economy. It offers educational programs that focus on three key content areas: entrepreneurship, work readiness, and financial literacy. **www.ja.org**

Mental Health Issues for Kids and Teens
Offers articles, games, and book reviews for children and adolescents interested in understanding mental health issues. Includes information on depression, ADHD, dealing with bullies, and disabilities **www.ncpamd.com**

Mind Over Matter
Helps young people learn about the effects of drug abuse on the body and the brain. **www.teens.drugabuse.gov**

The National Foundation for Teaching Entrepreneurship (NFTE)
Helps young people from low-income communities learn about business and develop their entrepreneurial skills. **www.nfte.com**

The National Mentoring Partnership
A national organization working to expand mentoring opportunities for young people. The Web site helps young people find a mentor. **www.mentoring.org**

SSC: Sierra Student Coalition
Offers environmental leadership training programs for high-school students in different cities across the United States. **www.ssc.org**

Summer Jobs

A great starting point for students looking for summer employment. Browse through the job postings, submit a résumé, or add yourself to the e-mail list to get job updates. **www.summerjobs.com**

Teen-Anon

Help for teens with drinking or drug problems. **www.teen-anon.com**

The Write Source

This site offers ideas for writing projects, examples of teen writing, and a chance to be published. **www.thewritesource.com**

Youth Communication

Youth Communication, founded in 1980, is a nonprofit youth development program located in New York City, whose mission is to teach writing, journalism, and leadership skills, and to make youth voices heard as widely as possible. Each year, 100 public high-school students write and illustrate Youth Communication's two award-winning teen magazines. The writers are a diverse group, including teens in foster care, recent immigrants, and low-income youth. Working with full-time professional editors, the writers may take several months to complete a single story. This process results in writing of uncommon depth and authenticity.

In addition to publishing magazines, Youth Communication has published more than 70 anthologies on topics teens consider most important, such as peer pressure, families, and improving their communities. Stories by teens at Youth Communication are also frequently reprinted in popular and professional magazines, from *CosmoGIRL!* to the *Harvard Educational Review.*

Youth Communication strives to serve three primary audiences: teen writers, teen readers, and educators.

▶▶ **Writers:** Writing for peers motivates teens to develop their literacy skills, meet deadlines, take individual responsibility, and work as a team to produce high-quality magazines.

▸▸ **Readers:** Teen readers report that reading their peers' stories makes them feel less isolated and more hopeful about the future. They also say that the stories give them information they can't get anywhere else and promote discussions with parents and other significant adults.

▸▸ **Educators:** Teachers and youth workers use Youth Communication publications to inspire reluctant readers and to broach difficult topics in safe and stimulating ways. They also report that reading our books and magazines show them what's really important to teens, which helps them establish better relations with their students and clients.

Youth Communication®
224 W. 29th Street, 2F.
New York, NY 10001
212-279-0708
www.youthcomm.org

Bibliography

SUCCESS for Teens includes real-life stories written by teens. Some stories are excerpts from books and magazines of the Youth Communication writing program, and are reprinted here with their permission. For more information on Youth Communcation, see Resources for Teens.

"The Crew from the Parking Lot," by Ferentz LaFargue, reprinted with permission from *Starting With I: Personal Essays by Teenagers*, Copyright 1997 by Youth Communication/New York Center, Inc., Persea Books, Inc.

"Hiding My Talent No More," by Jesselin Rodriguez, reprinted with permission from *We're Better Than We Think: Teens Write About Surviving Middle School*, Copyright 2007 by Youth Communication/New York Center, Inc.

"Girl Stop Frontin'," by Chantel Clark, reprinted with permission from *Real Stories, Real Teens*, Copyright 2007 by Youth Communication/New York Center, Inc.

"College Can Be Hell," by Tamecka Crawford, reprinted with permission from *The Struggle to Be Strong*, Copyright 2000 by Youth Communication and Project Resilience, Free Spirit Publishing.

"Why I Stopped Being Shy," by Kesly Coba, reprinted with permission from *New Youth Connections*, November/December, 1998, Youth Communication/New York Center, Inc.

"Going for It," by Anonymous, reprinted with permission from *New Youth Connections*, May/June, 1996, Youth Communication/New York Center, Inc.

"In the Driver's Seat: Setting Goals Gets You on the Road. Here's How to Get Going," by Xavier Reyes, reprinted with permission from *Do You Have What It Takes? A Comprehensive Guide to Success After Foster Care*, Copyright 1997 by Youth Communication.

"Keep the Future in Mind," by Ralph Tarrant, reprinted with permission from *Represent*, July/August, 1998, Youth Communication/New York Center, Inc.

"Why Do We Love Labels?" by Patricia D. Rogers, reprinted with permission from *New Youth Connections*, December, 2005, Youth Communication/New York Center, Inc.

"Confessions of a Shopaholic," by Jeremiah Spears, reprinted with permission from *Represent*, March/April, 2000, Youth Communication/ New York Center, Inc.

"My Journal Saved My Life," by Anonymous, reprinted with permission from *Fighting the Monster*, Copyright 2004 by Youth Communication/New York Center, Inc.

Acknowledgments

The editors of *SUCCESS for Teens* would like to thank:

JEFF OLSON, for introducing his good friend, Stuart Johnson, to the slight edge philosophy and for his many years of teaching, refining, and educating millions on it;

JOHN DAVID MANN, for helping Jeff with the manuscript of his best-selling book, *The Slight Edge*;

AL DESETTA and John David Mann, for working with the SUCCESS Foundation on the preparation of this book's manuscript;

KEITH HEFNER and the staff at YOUTH COMMUNICATION in New York for their generosity in making available many of the teen stories in this book; and

The millions of people who have successfully applied the slight edge philosophy to their lives.